RIVER

OF

WORDS

RIVER OF WORDS

YOUNG POETS AND ARTISTS

on the

NATURE OF THINGS

Edited by

PAMELA MICHAEL

Introduced by

ROBERT HASS

MILKWEED EDITIONS

Published 2008 by Milkweed Editions

Cover design by Brad Norr Design
Front cover art, "River of Words,"
 by Lim Yi Fan, age 11
Front flap art, "River of Words,"
 by Angelina Ooi Wei Wei, age 11
Back cover art (detail), "Summer Showers,"
 by Loren Kim, age 15
Author photo by Nora Ericson
Interior design by Cathy Spengler
The text of this book is set in LinoLetter.
08 09 10 11 12 5 4 3 2 1
First Edition

Milkweed Editions, a nonprofit publisher, gratefully
acknowledges sustaining support from Anonymous;
Emilie and Henry Buchwald; the Bush Foundation;
the Patrick and Aimee Butler Family Foundation;
CarVal Investors; the Dougherty Family Foundation;
the Ecolab Foundation; the General Mills Foundation; the Claire Giannini Fund; John and Joanne
Gordon; William and Jeanne Grandy; the Jerome
Foundation; Dorothy Kaplan Light and Ernest Light;
Constance B. Kunin; Marshall BankFirst Corp.;
Sanders and Tasha Marvin; the May Department
Stores Company Foundation; the McKnight Foundation; a grant from the Minnesota State Arts Board,
through an appropriation by the Minnesota State
Legislature, a grant from the National Endowment
for the Arts, and private funders; an award from the
National Endowment for the Arts, which believes that
a great nation deserves great art; the Navarre Corporation; Debbie Reynolds; the Starbucks Foundation;
the St. Paul Travelers Foundation; Ellen and Sheldon
Sturgis; the Target Foundation; the Gertrude Sexton
Thompson Charitable Trust (George R. A. Johnson,
Trustee); the James R. Thorpe Foundation; the Toro
Foundation; Moira and John Turner; United Parcel
Service; Joanne and Phil Von Blon; Kathleen and Bill
Wanner; Serene and Christopher Warren; the W. M.
Foundation; and the Xcel Energy Foundation.

Library of Congress Cataloging-in-Publication Data
 River of words : young poets and artists on
the nature of things / edited by Pamela Michael ;
introduced by Robert Hass. — 1st ed.
  p. cm.
 Includes Index
 ISBN 978-1-57131-680-6 (pbk. : alk. paper)
 ISBN 978-1-57131-685-1 (hardcover : alk. paper)
 1. Water—Juvenile poetry. 2. Children's poetry,
American. 3. Young adult poetry, American.
4. Water in art. I. Michael, Pamela.
 PS595.W374R588 2008
 811.008′036—dc22
                                    2007046483

This book is printed on acid-free paper.
Printed in Canada

MINNESOTA
STATE ARTS BOARD

NATIONAL
ENDOWMENT
FOR THE ARTS
A great nation
deserves great art.

TARGET.

In Loving Memory of Sanford Lyne

(1946–2007)

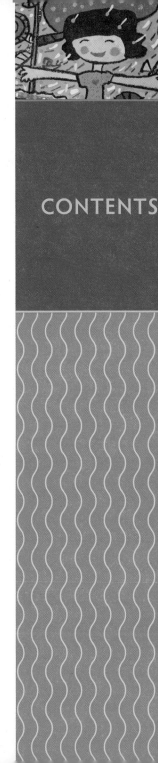

CONTENTS

*E*very February the River of Words office fills to the rafters with packages sent in by children and teachers. The packages contain poems, paintings, and drawings that describe with uncommon clarity and power the landscapes and lives of young people around the world. The first piles of mail cover all the available horizontal surfaces—shelves, tables, desktops—in our sixteen-hundred-square-foot space in a 1913 mattress factory turned artisan complex. Subsequent deliveries fill teetering towers of milk crates. Neighbors stop by to marvel. It's an exciting and exhausting time for us.

Reading the mail at "contest time" each year is one of the best parts of my job as director of River of Words. In a one-month flurry I select a couple hundred entries out of the thousands we receive, from which Robert Hass, Thacher Hurd, and I choose each year's winners. Our free international youth poetry and art contest has become, in twelve years, the largest in the world. We receive tens of thousands of entries annually from classrooms in Washington, DC, to Richmond, California; 4-H clubs in Iowa; Wildlife Clubs in Kenya; refugee camps in Pakistan; homeschoolers; Girl Scout troops; from kids in summer camps, after-school programs, and juvenile detention. Each submission we receive— even those not selected for this book—is remarkable for its unique and diverse interpretation of the places and times in which we live.

As you will see in the pages of this book, the world's children are perhaps its most truthful and sensitive observers. With the help of our *Watershed Explorer* curriculum and the guidance of educators dedicated to providing their students with learning opportunities that connect them to local landscapes and the natural world, many children—through their poetry and art—are helping all of us see and understand the earth in new ways. In doing so they are learning about themselves and their language, and making sense of the world around them. All with just paper and pencil, open eyes, ears—and hearts.

The volume and variety of work I review every year reveals some startling truths. (A colleague pointed out to me recently that

I probably see more children's art and poetry than anyone in the world; it's a great privilege, joy, and responsibility.) Several years ago I started noticing that our entries seemed to have a theme (in addition to the stated contest theme of "watersheds") running through them each year, as if all the kids in the world somehow communicated with each other and decided to depict, say, tree hollows with small creatures peering out, as in 1999 when it seemed that every other painting contained such an image. Another year, it was snow-capped mountains. Another, the word "everlasting."

Once I started paying attention to this curious phenomenon, deeper and more meaningful patterns emerged. In 2002, while some poems directly addressed the previous year's World Trade Center tragedy, thousands more did so obliquely. Poem after poem contained words like *grief, tears, sorrow, death, plummet,* and *loss.* After the 2003 invasion of Iraq, our poetry entries were full of war imagery. Again, few poems dealt directly with the war; rather, beetles battled, storms raged, and rain pounded as nature and creatures ravaged and fought violently in our children's imaginations. The 2004 Indian Ocean tsunami seemed to have an especially profound impact on children's psyches, perhaps because of the primal fear associated with drowning. Images of being engulfed by a giant wave continue to appear in both our poetry and art submissions. The fear lingers.

Our 2007 entries were particularly troubling. I often found myself crying as I read through poems with themes of fear, rage, and confusion, not surprising in a time of world upheaval. That art and poetry might provide a means for children to express their fears is some consolation. Wallace Stevens wrote that the poet's role is to "help people live their lives." Exploring difficult issues, both global and personal, not only nurtures those who read these poems but also affords comfort and perspective to the creators.

Despite a daily diet of calamity, young people find much to celebrate in the world around them. They are playful, inventive, candid, and surprising. Their work vibrates with wonder and joy. And they love to read poetry written by other young people. Our annual anthologies of art and poetry are used by many teachers to inspire their students with examples of excellence that they can relate to their lives. We've seen the fruits of such modeling over the years: the 1999 poem "Dear Night," (page 226) inspired "Dear Aquarius," (page 242) in 2000, and both informed "Dear Stars," (page 92) in 2002.

~~~~~~~~~~~~~~~~

When Robert Hass and I created River of Words in 1995, we hoped that focusing students' attention on local watersheds—on their own home grounds—would give them an informed understanding of place that would help them grow into active citizens. We sought to nurture creativity and promote the idea that while not everyone can be an artist, everyone can be artistic. We tried to add elements of wonder, discovery, interpretation, dexterity, and surprise to learning. Our small and hopeful idea has grown into a program that trains hundreds of teachers each year and touches the lives of tens of thousands of children annually. As we had hoped in our activist hearts, River of Words is helping to build community partnerships between schools, businesses, grassroots groups, and government agencies, and also promoting collaboration among teachers within schools.

And, to be sure, it is the legions of creative, dedicated educators who have made River of Words such a successful tool for learning. Working with classroom teachers, Scout leaders, docents, and other youth leaders in our professional development workshops over the last decade has enriched my life and River of Words' programs beyond measure. While we have coordinators in many states— most notably Petey Giroux at the Georgia Department of Natural Resources, who has embedded River of Words in schools and nature centers throughout her state—it is typically an individual teacher who brings our environmental and arts curriculum into a classroom then watches students blossom with creativity, often igniting other students' and teachers' imaginations as well. Before long, the entire school and community are cleaning up a creek, publishing poetry booklets or putting on a watershed festival. River of Words is designed to be a catalyst for such activities, allowing local resources, needs, and circumstances to guide the shape of the program. Accordingly, River of Words looks very different on the island of Mt. Desert, Maine than it does in California Central Valley's Merced County.

It is at the local level that River of Words is most visible, vibrant, and effective. We at the national headquarters in northern California have face-to-face contact with only a fraction of the children our program reaches; indeed, about fifteen percent of them live outside the US—in Bangladesh, Indonesia, Ukraine, India, Malaysia, China, Azerbaijan, Afghanistan, England, Zimbabwe, and elsewhere. So it is only through their poetry and art that we get to know most of the children. Those few we are privileged to meet in person—in classroom visits or at our award ceremonies in Washington, DC, and San Francisco—leave an indelible mark. Their stories remind us of the power of the creative act and community recognition to transform lives.

~~~~~~~~~~~~~~

Of all the children I have met through River of Words, perhaps none has affected me as much as Jane Jiang, an only child of Chinese immigrants, whose development as a poet we have witnessed from the age of nine, when she started entering the River of Words contest. She is now in her sophomore year of college. Jane's poetry—nurtured not only by River of Words but also by an extraordinary teacher at Lakeside School in Seattle, Alicia Hokanson (our 2003 Teacher of the Year)—is a disarming and skillful blend of wisdom and youthfulness. After being chosen a national finalist several times, she won the Grand Prize in 2002 and went on to publish a book of her own poems while still in high school.

Her poem "Fledgling," which follows, is perhaps one of the best coming-of-age poem ever written, a visceral dispatch from the intricate, jangling frontiers of adolescence. It has been my honor and pleasure to watch Jane and countless other young people grow as artists, citizens and empathetic human beings over the years. And now, in these pages, the pleasure will be yours, too.

~~~~~~~~~~~~~~~~~~~~

FLEDGLING

I remember or imagine fighting
An implacability of sky;
Chafing against being child, being young
Resistant and unpliant against
The softest upbringing, still begging to be released;
This inner hurricane my ribcage cannot dam,
Wild young hurricane riding astride and tearing at the mane
      of the beast.

Chafing, until the final moment when suddenly the chained friction
Against our skin seems a blessing;
Then chastened and reproved we cling
And peer hesitant over the edge into the great abyss,
And do not wish to leave.
And do not wish to leave.
And pray to stay,
Darkly, in the cowardly pits of our young, flailing hearts;
Being not yet burnt but fearing the lick of heat, retract
Our fingers and retreat.

It reminds me. I found a nest of newborn birds once
In the upper reaches of my grandma's cherry tree
I thought them exceedingly ugly, awkward ungainly things
Heads tilted at funny angles, feathers slick with sweat or grease.

That summer—I might have been eight—I watched them
        grow anyway,
Ugly birds are better than no birds at all,
Watched the damp, stiff spines ease and spread to feathered wings,
Saw the pinions extend to flight,
Remember one day when the strawberries were ripening
And I at eight already an ersatz poet—remember watching
The mother bird diving, swinging great dizzy loops around the
Deep new green of summer cherry leaves
And looping, looping, resting sometimes and pausing
As if begging fledglings to follow and to take leave.

What a bite the dusky summer air must have held,
To explain the hesitation of those fledgling birds!
And when finally one emerged,
What trembling in its feathers!
In the first, most dangerous downward swerve.

And what a clattering sits now in my heart.
Ten thousand tinny high-hats clashing,
Ten thousand crazed handkerchiefs drifting
Attesting to the insanity of this wind.

What a roaring in my ears!
What an emptiness in my throat,
Gaping with each fresh breath, as if a threat
To consume me like a black hole from within.

What an eagerness to be gone, to prove
The unprovable, even to play a martyr to the waiting crowds!
What a war fought backward and forward,
The blood of minutes staining the space between,
Step forward and step back; too much to think.

What a burning to shout
That we are all grown up now, we are too far gone now,
Kites on an updraft with the string well cut!
Dizzying vertigo swirling around our empty knees
As the figures below us floating recede
Elemental dispersion, bonds stretched to breaking thin,
Those who love us whispering come back,
Back, back again.

What a taut stretching there was in my heart
As I sat on my knees at eight, by the tree,
Watching the first timid bird plummet downwards.
It dropped like a pebble thrown too high against
A red-streaked sunset sky.
I bit dry lips, thought its neck might break
A split second before it seemed to wake.
Then curved a wild and inarticulate arc
And landed, as if by miracle, on twiggy feet.
I felt my squeezed heart in every gasping beat.

And poised now, girl-child, child-woman,
Perched on the edge of flight, perched
With my brethren around me, each of us pleading,
Begging a step forward and a step back,
Indecisive moments staining the minutes ticking in our minds.

Go now. We'll take this plunge together:
One flock of still-damp feathers straining toward the burning of the
light:
So singe the edges of your wings.
Dare the flame, go, go, on the updraft while it lasts,
Take me with you, and you with me—
We go now in a great dispersing fleet
To burn and plummet, and carve our own arcs
Through implacable skies.

~ *Jane S. Jiang, Bellevue, Washington*

*This poem was written and performed for Jane's graduation from Lake-
side School in Seattle in 2006. More of her poems can be found on pages
82, 92, and 98 of this book.*

*T*he charm of these poems, their vividness and variety, humor and poignancy and surprising depths, do not need to be encumbered by an introduction. Nicholas Sanz-Gould and Rebecca Givens and Jane Jiang and the dozens of other young poets in this book speak very much for themselves. In fact, the idea of River of Words was to encourage young people to speak for themselves, and to speak about the geographies they know and to mirror them back, in this way, to their communities. Our thought was that because children are still out playing in the world most adults have set aside for offices and shops they would have the power to remind us not only of the task of stewardship but of what it is in the world and ourselves we are stewarding. A second thought was that encouraging, drawing attention to, and rewarding the work children do would be of some help to the dedicated teachers and educators in our schools, museums of natural history, and state and national parks who are trying to keep environmental education on the agenda. The poet's phrase for what we were hoping to focus here belongs to William Wordsworth. He called it "the most watchful power of love."

So, though the poems don't require an introduction, for readers, young people coming to poetry, teachers, and readers of poetry curious about what these children can do, here are three ideas that have served us over the years as contexts for thinking about these poems and the project River of Words proposes. The first has to do with children and art, the second with children and stewardship, the third with the idea of watersheds.

1. CHILDREN AND ART

In her wonderful book *Children's Art* (University of California Press, 1957), Pia Lindstrom observes that very young children, when they are making paintings, often don't remember afterward which of the paintings is theirs. She writes,

The picture seems to be only a byproduct of the main interest,
the act *of painting. Expressing their feeling-thought about some*
happening lived or imagined is one of the main uses of art work
to children of four or five, but this procedure of 'acting-out' a dra-
matic event is still beyond many of the two- and three-year-olds.
For them, thinking and feeling seem to be directly related to the
physical activity going on rather than to mental activity concerned
with concepts to be expressed. Their incidental chatter to them-
selves and each other is not so important as their own perfor-
mance of an act of skill. They enjoy the 'power of being the cause.'

I have loved that last sentence ever since I first read it. And I
think that what it says is as true of adult artists as it is of two- and
three-year-olds. A national survey some years ago asked American
schoolchildren if they were "mainly happy or mainly worried." I was
interested and dismayed to read that more of them—fourth graders,
I think—reported that they were worried rather than happy. This
might be a developmental fact, that their responses came from the
onset of a sense of responsibility that is also a sense of self, and in
that way not a bad sign. Nevertheless when the survey asked them
what they were worried about, the principal answers were AIDS and
pollution, subjects about which they could not have known very much,
that their alert young antennae must have picked up from the culture
at large. There are practical steps, of course, that children and adults
can take to feel less powerless about the condition of the world, but in
this way, especially with the young, I think art is a mighty power, and
it is important that they learn it, and are encouraged to learn it, early.
The words of a poet again, this time Gerard Manley Hopkins:

Each mortal thing does one thing and the same:
Deals out that being indoors each one dwells;
Selves—goes itself; myself it speaks and spells
Crying What I do is me; for that I came.

2. CHILDREN AND STEWARDSHIP

"No important change in ethics was ever accomplished without an internal change in our intellectual emphasis, loyalties, affections, and convictions. The proof that conservation has not yet touched the foundations of conduct lies in the fact that philosophy and religion have not yet heard of it," Aldo Leopold writes in *Sand Country Almanac*. A little later in the book, he comes out in a slightly different way: "It is inconceivable to me that an ethical relation to land can exist without love, respect, and admiration for land, and a high regard for its value." And by "land," he says, he means not just soil but "a fountain of energy flowing through the circuit of soils, plants, and animals."

One of our basic ideas lies here. We are not apt to be very effective caretakers of anything that we don't come to know and understand, and we are not apt to come to know and understand anything that hasn't awakened our curiosity or fascination. It's clear enough at the beginning of the twenty-first century that the fates of almost all the species of plants and animals, the biota of the earth, forests and grasslands, tundra and glacial bays, mangrove swamps and deserts have come into the hands of human beings. And so an education in ecological citizenship has become an international necessity, especially in the developed countries that use so many of the world's resources. And it's pretty clear, or it ought to be, that the beginnings of that education lie in the natural energy, curiosity, and alertness of children and in the passion to pass on a world that commits people to the vocation of teaching.

I think human beings only gradually evolved, for reasons of efficiency, our present tendency to sort out song-making and image-making from the learning of a culture's lore about the earth and the water and the stars. Our children are educated in a system that tends to divide art and music (when they are taught at all) and writing on the one hand, and natural history and social history and science, into distinctly different disciplines and different parts of the day. But they are all activities that begin in observation and imagination, and stewardship of the earth is going to require both. Also, the energy of art is an aspect of the energy that flows through a place. The children who watch plants grow know very well that they are growing, too. And an expression of the energy and rhythm of that experience is also a kind of knowing. Children can be quizzed on the life cycle of salmon; they are apt to know it better and feel it more deeply if they have also danced it, or caught the rhythm of it in words or color or movement.

We think these poems are, among other things, evidence of this power in children and of the remarkable work being done by teachers in many of our educational institutions, even though the culture has not yet really taken on the task of education in stewardship, has in fact been in denial about the need.

3. THE IDEA OF A WATERSHED

In his wonderful essay "Coming Into a Watershed," from *A Place in Space,* Gary Snyder gives us, with a characteristic elegance of mind, a definition.

> *A watershed is a marvelous thing to consider: this process of rain falling, streams flowing, and oceans evaporating causes every molecule on earth to make the complete trip once every two million years. The surface is carved into watersheds—a kind of familial branching, a chart of relationship, and a definition of place. The watershed is the first and last nations whose boundaries, though subtle shifting, are unarguable. Races of birds, subspecies of trees, and types of hats or rain gear often go by watershed. [And] we who live in terms of centuries rather than millions of years must hold the watershed and its communities together, so our children might enjoy the clear water and the fresh life of this landscape we have chosen.*

He goes on to speak of his own watershed in California:

The water cycle includes our springs and wells, our Sierra snow-pack, our irrigation canals, our car wash, and the spring salmon run. It's the spring peeper in the pond and the acorn woodpecker chattering in a snag. The watershed is beyond the dichotomies of orderly/disorderly, for its forms are free but somehow inevitable. The life that comes to flourish within it constitutes the first kind of community.

This is the reason why the focus of River of Words was, from the start, watersheds. The place to begin, we felt, was not a generalized stewardship of the earth or an intellectual grasp on the energy flows of an ecosystem or lists of endangered species or, for that matter, the technological achievements of our beginning science of restoration, but their feel for the places where they live. Asking them to think in terms of watersheds is a way of connecting what they already know from their vivid, lively, daily experience of their weather and their place to the idea of the bioregion and human and biotic community they are part of. It is also a way of recommending to teachers—though we've found over twelve years that the teachers were way ahead of us, even though the schools and the schools of education and the educational reforms of politicians have done not very much to encourage them—that a good way to do art, writing, natural history and social history in the classroom is to root it in local, hands-on experience and observation. One of our early posters for the art and poetry contest read, "Do you know your ecological address?" That was the idea, and the poems that follow are some of the answers to that question.

RIVER
OF
WORDS

MY NAME IS ELIJAH

Waterfalls told me hello today.
The river also talked.
She wanted me to know
that my name
was important.
My name is Elijah.
I am a friend of the river.

~ *Elijah Soza, age 5*

SAD SUN

Oh sun. Oh sun.
Oh sun. How does
it feel to be
blocked by the
dark dark clouds?

Oh child
it doesn't really
feel bad at all
not at all not at
all not at all.

~ *Nicholas Sanz-Gould, age 6*

RAIN FEELING

The nap time rain
sings lullabies
and throws all kinds
of flowers on your head
shimmering stars
and rainbows

~

Jessica Mozes, age 7

When I'm happy
100 deer
Jump over the sun
When I laugh
100 bears
Laugh with me

~ *Angela Meza, age 6*

BEST BEAR
Nicky Witty, age 8

I/YO

I . . .
I am paper without a drawing.
I want people to write on me.
I know all the kinds of ink in the world.
I come from trees.
I have seen all the animals of the forest.

Yo . . .
Yo soy papel sin escritura.
Yo quiero que las personas escriban en mí.
Yo sé todos los tipos de tinta en el mundo.
Yo vengo de los árboles.
Yo he visto todos los animales en el bosque.

~ *Amelia Archer, age 7*

IF I WERE IN CHARGE OF THE WORLD . . .

If I were in charge of the world
I'd cancel war, guns, animal abuse, and also
homework.

If I were in charge of the world
There would be free money, food, and
There would be lots of popcorn.

If I were in charge of the world
There would not be violence, cigarettes, alcohol
or plane crashes.

~ *Francisco Javier Piñeda, age 7*

COYOTE

Cotton coat of many colors
OWW oww he goes
Yowling every night.
Other coyotes come to play
Eyes as bright as the moon.

~ *Kathryn Moffett, age 8*

NATURE

Slithering on a dirt path,
A green snake rushes to safety.
Water is splashing, trees are whooshing.
Grass grows wild in the meadow.
Chirping, a robin sits in a tree,
Red and black, looking down at me.
The sun floats down, down, down.
I can see the moon's white eye.

~ *Richard Moala, age 9*

FISH

Swimming in the river,
Curving her small, shining body
Like shimmering stars swimming back
Into the deep sea
Being the fish of joy.

~ *Ella Schoefer-Wulf, age 9*

THERE IS A DARK RIVER

There is a dark river
In the gutter of the street
In front of my school.
It was born in the rain
And isn't flowing anymore.
It's sort of sad
With drops of gasoline
And a red wrapper
Some kid tossed
After eating a candy.
But although it's sad and filthy
It carries the shadow of my face
The tattered clouds
And in white and black
The whole sky.

HAY UN RÍO OSCURO

En la alcantarilla de la calle
En frente de mi escuela.
Nació de la lluvia
Y ya no corre más.
Se queda triste
Con gotas de gasolina
Y un papel rojo
Que tiró un niño
Después de comer un dulce.
Pero aun triste y sucio
Lleva la sombra de mi cara
Las nubes andrajosas
Y en blanco y negro
Todo el cielo.

~ *Michelle Díaz Garza, age 9*
& Rosa Baum, age 9

25

THIS PLACE

The creek runs past
a fallen grandmother
bay tree

Over stones
smoothed
by the centuries

The ripples
seem to be
everlasting

A buckeye leaf
floats down
the creek

While the wrentit sings
and the sword fern
stands guard

Five-finger ferns
peek
over the edge

The love of this place
is like
a child's heart.

~ *Tobi Earnheart-Gold, age 9*

I am the web of a spider.
I am as sticky as the

Golden bees' honey. The thin
Twine is no thinner than me.

The falling of dew, like
The rain of spring, drips

Off me, slowly and
Surely like the

Beating of the mocking
Bird's wing. Twisting and

Turning like the curls
Of my sister Jenna's hair

Am I. With much ease
I shine in the golden

Sun. Every day I worry

The finger will shatter
Me. But I smile at the sight

Of the fly.

~ *Leanne Brotsky, age 9*

I AM

You may think
I am a shadow,
But inside
I am a sun.

~

Damia Gates, age 9

TO MY PARENTS

Thanks
to my parents
who have given
me expression so
I can wake my red heart.

Gracias
a mis papas
que me han dado
expresión para
despertarme el corazón rojo.

~ *Luis Manuel Zamora, age 9*

ODE TO WATER

To the water,
that fills the oceans,
that marries the earth,
they fly,
they fly together to the planets
that tell the rain to rain.

To the water,
that rides the wind,
that's smarter than a book,
that can do anything,
for the dead to the living.

To the water,
fast,
cold,
that can swallow you in one gulp,
that slowly
turns into a creek,
that laughs when it falls.

To the water,
that gave me life.

ODA AL AGUA

Al agua,
que llena los océanos,
que se casa con la tierra,
vuela,
vuelan los dos a los planetas,
que dice a la lluvia a llover.

Al agua,
que monta el viento,
que es más inteligente que un libro,
que puede ser todo,
a los muertos hasta los vivos.

Al agua,
rápida,
fría,
que te puede comer en un bocado,
que lentamente
se hace un riachuelo,
que ríe mientras se cae.

Al agua,
que me ha dado vida.

~ *Lydia Elías, age 9*

SPRING ON MOUNT TAMALPAIS

    The misty breeze
pushing against my rosy, cold-nipped
nose,
      the crisp trees frosty from
the night, the swaying
flowers
      that just broke
      into bloom, the mossy hills crinkled in the
wind
      the curled ferns
unrolled to
      meet the
        early morning
air.

~ *Zoe Goldberg, age 9*

BUTTERFLY

Voice #1	*Voice #2*
I used to be a caterpillar	
	caterpillar
munching leaves with unquenchable hunger	mmmmmmmmmm *(softly)*
	hunger
then a long sleep	then a long sleep
	I
awoke	awoke
	examining myself in
a drop of dew	a drop of dew
	to find I was
different	different

                              now I stand
                              basking in the sun
                              preparing

                              for
preparing   flight

for

                              FLIGHT
FLIGHT

~ *Amanda Ditmore, age 10*

The moon voice
shouts out
brilliant twilight
through acres of
black sky

~

Luis Castillo, age 10

I FOUND A LITTLE PART OF ME . . .

In the river
I found a little part of me
In the river
my face reflects
In the river
my shadow appears
In the river
my shadow is black
and looks bigger than me.

ENCONTRÉ UN POCO DE MÍ . . .

En el río
encontré un poco de mí
En el río
se refleja me rostro
En el río
me sombra se veía
En el rio
la sombra era negra
y se ve mas grande que yo.

~ *Jonathan García de Alba, age 10*

AWAY

Blow me away . . .
make me fly freely like a bird in a cloud
carry me away . . .

Fly to the end of the sky
where time flies with me
blow me away . . .

Show me the soul of the sky
where I will plummet down on a swift current
carry me away . . .

Tell me what the world wants of me
move me then
carry me away . . .

Away from the depths of night
to shimmering fog that resembles heavenly clouds to
blow me away . . .
carry me away . . .

And do nothing to stop me here
And do nothing to change me here
And do nothing to keep me here
And push me into the
depths of morning fog to show me
what I can be

~ *Jenna Archer, age 10*

ODE TO THE STRAWBERRY

O strawberry
Forgive me because
You have so many
Freckles on your face
But I couldn't
Bear it and I ate
You in one bite
And locked you up
In my stomach
So warm and filthy.

ODA A LA FRESA

O fresa
Perdóname por
Si tienes muchas
Pecas en tu cara
Pero yo no pude
Aguantar y te
Comí en un mordisco
Y te encerré
En mi estómago
Caliente y sucio

~ *Cinthia Martínez, age 10*

BERRY FALLS

Spraying sounds of crashing water   speeding over slick,

                mossy rocks seep

                          into my ears. Flittering droplets

          tickle my   face and

     I can almost   taste the calm.

~ *Malcolm Kim, age 10*

SPRING TIME
Elizabeth Elaine Au, age 13

SKY

I am the sky.
I cover the earth like a giant blanket.
Clouds float
                    below me like
a school of
                    silvery
                    fish.
I protect the earth from the dark
freeze of space and the hot singe of
the sun.

I am the sky.

~ *Zachary Postone, age 10*

SPIDER

Oh delicate being
legs like silky strands reflecting the
sun
your web sprinkled with
crystal beads after the
rain.
Your body a black
pearl
shining in the sun.
Your eyes fiery
sparks
shimmering in the night.
Oh delicate being
weave your silver
strands of
light.

~ *Henry Whittaker, age 10*

MAPLE

Oh maple
maple maple
your leaves
bottled
up with
joy
ready to
burst off and
float
riding the winds
grass
tickling your
crinkled
belly

~

Ciro Podany, age 11

THE FLAME

The flame of orange persimmon collides
with the dark of the pomegranate
as the seeds circle the thing of
change they learn how the inside
is the outside. Within an apple of rust
is a seed that is born and how the hill
is alive and dead at the same time.
As the rattle of the snake is the
fate of the tree and if the mouse
steps here the bird will live and
if it does not the bird will die.
And the wind in the tree is
nothing.

~ *Forrest Ambruster, age 11*

SNOW

As the moonstone
lace was falling
whose soul tiptoed
through the forest?
Which song fluttered
through the wood?
When the snow
falls next winter
which secret will
it bring?

~ *Elsinore Smidth-Carabetta, age 11*

SEASONS

The seasons change
so much for the plum tree
one day with leaves
and another
without.

~

Derek Wyant, age 11

The wind is talking to me.
It's telling me a secret.
A secret about the clouds.

El viento me está hablando.
Me está diciendo un secreto.
Un secreto de las nubes.

~ *Kimberly Guzmán, age 12*

CHUCKWALLA
(Lizard of the Canyon)

orange
as the tropical
sun,
black
rings as black
as the bone
rings of
death
white
as the
radiant whispers of
the moon.

old
as the earth,
young
as the
stars,
as sleek
as the
river where
I met
them.

~

Jeffrey Herbertson, age 12

UNTITLED
Antoaneta Mitkova Demireva, age 15

47

SWIM IN ME

swim in me
            i'm yours
                        my waves
                                    yours
                                                my rivers
                                                    yours
                                                    my streams
                                                    yours
                                                my creeks
                                    yours
            my lakes
yours
my ponds
yours
            my rain
                        yours
                                    my clouds
                        yours
            swim in me

            i'm yours

                        ~

Gracie Jordan, age 12

48

THE RIVER

Slow as mud,
Fast as lightning.
Gentle, soothing,
Violent, frightening.

The earth's blood,
A stone's cool breath.
Warm with life,
Cold as death.

A path well known,
To an unknown world.
Near yet distant,
Straight then curled.

As silent as a shadow,
Or louder than a storm.
An eternal shape,
With temporary form.

A river flows forever,
Wild, strong and free.
Until it reaches its goal,
And runs into the sea.

~

Taylor V. Hattori, age 12

TIME CHANGES EVERYTHING

Gritty creeky waterway.
Chilly air wraps the silence.
Bird tracks impress me.
The ancient oak dangles its roots over the water.
Times changes everything.

~ *Dillon York, age 12*

THE MILLIONTH CIRCLE

Rippling outward
In
Twinkling vibrations
Flickering under the silent
Orb of the moon
The stars giddy
With the sight of countless circles
The fish smile
A mere kiss can cause
A million circles

~

Leia Sandmann, age 12

Cinnamon thistles,
spicy paprika autumn.
Wool socks,
caterpillar curled in the
gray soil where cabbage once grew.
Withered wet grass
humming in the
bitter bite of breeze.
Prickly milkweed
and silken clover.
A gypsy moth twirls by.
Violet beads trickle
down from whispering tendrils,
the shed skins of rain clouds.
Iced cranberry
roses,
their crimson petals trapped in frostbite.
The freckles of mist, the
flecks of topaz,
the gray mist of sea.

~ *Nicole Grinsell, age 12*

THE LEVEE

The asphalt is rough
Uneven and crude
Rocks piled up against the
     levee wall
With dirt and small, scrubby
     plants
Hemlock and horsetail
Struggling to grow
Among the beer cans
And
Plastic Pepsi bottles
On the other side
I see the Pajaro River
It's that time of year
Spring
When the grass grows
To cover the trash
That is strewn among
     the poppies and vetch

There's graffiti on the bridge
Tags . . . in garish, faded colors
And I pretend I don't see
The blankets and sleeping bags
Dirty and wrinkled
Spread under the bridge
Does someone live there?
What do they do
When the river runs high and brown?
Flowing like time like brown sand
Through the thin neck of an hourglass
The river flows
Through a wide path of stone, sand
     and mud banks
Carving history
As time flows

~ *Camila Pérez, age 12*

THROUGH THE LENS

Flirting shadows
A little breeze
Through thick beams of metal
Rusty, red, hard with age
The trestle stands still
100,000 frames of life,
Of stories
Revolving/orbiting
Surrounding it
Graffiti, tags, a secret language
Written with spray paint and
      peppered with obscenities

Bouncing, glancing, trembling
      beams of light
Reflecting off
The still brown water
Standing stagnant beneath
      the bridge
Mirror, mirror, river small
Who's the dirtiest of all?

I'm knotted, snarled, crissed and
      crossed, confused and spinning
Simply, simply
Trying to see it all at once
Asphalt cracked, bags, rags
Scattered evidence of a will to survive
In another world, the edge, the door
Where green shines through murky haze
Of brown, of scum, of dust, of muck of
      grime of
100 weary years of time
Woven all across the river
And
I'm trying to catch it
Glimpse it, snatch it
Through
A camera lens

~ *Camila Pérez, age 13*

MISS RIVER
Alina Ivchenko, age 12

BOBCAT

The hushed lavender light of
evening
rustles over the sun-bleached
hillsides of early autumn
The soft wind
ripples between my fingers
From the fading
depths
of the hills,
a warm shadow rolls toward me
Her velvet paws crinkle
the grass, her eyes glaze
my face,
with the wisdom of the
ancient oak tree,
the song of the harvest moon
and the perfume of the
shy wildflowers.

~ *Elsinore Smidth-Carabetta, age 13*

56

PEARLS FROM ABOVE

Punching the ground
With strong, powerful thumps
Pouring out of the sky
Clear, immaculate pearls
Each finds a way to the ground
Millions and millions
Try to slide their way through
Some collect in a group
Float together across the land
Pick up passengers along the way:
Slops of mud
Goopy oil
Bits of leaves
Tiny pebbles
All work together
To fight the heavy wind
Pearls turn to coffee
Mud disappears
Oil sinks to the bottom
Each a part of the other
Lost in a world of debris and strangers

~ *Karolinka Tekiela, age 13*

ROYAL OAKS

Redwood

Moist mossy floors
sprinkled with soft white mushrooms
and gentle green ferns
A small stream flows by with trout
swimming to the ocean

Slough

Salt-stained water
lined with pickleweed and old algae where
tiny green crabs can hide from hungry birds

Meadow

Fresh green grass damp with morning dew
A hawk glides lazily over a quiet pond
filled with water lilies and speckled frogs

I climb the redwood tree next to the stream
I catch the green crabs hiding under the pickleweed
I lie on the grass next to the pond listening to frogs
       sing to the twilight

This is where I live

~ *Lauren Anderson, age 13*

I don't think you understand
The beauty that is darkness
The overdone flamboyance
          of light
Do you realize
You take for granted
The absence of light?
Velvety blue black
And a purple undertone
Subtle colors are under the
          layers of night
They make stifled sounds
          underneath
The pitch black
Full petals grace my green shaft
Green for life,
Violet for majesty,
Black for sleeping passions
Round and full, mature and
          blossomed
Eye-catching amidst gaudy sky,
Sun
And fire-painted little flowers

Richness in the dark should
          draw you in
Voluptuous petals seem as though
          they beckon to you
Ready to wrap around you
Lead you into their world of eternal
          sleep
The dark is restful
Soothing to the eye
The eye that is burned by red and
          yellow roses
And the dancing baby blue of the sky
The sky's dance makes you tired,
          doesn't it?
Let the darkness hold you . . .
Let it own you for just one long
Night . . .

~   *Adriane Pontecorvo, age 13*

Inspired by Georgia O'Keefe's
"Black and Purple Petunias"

ODE TO OLD TOMATILLO

damaged tomatillo
a shell of crumpled population
surrounds it
like a cocoon with no caterpillar
attracts no attention, unlike the other
beautiful plants in the garden
it's like a green veiny comet
stopped in time
in spring it was bright and youthful
it has seen and known many secrets
shhh

~ *Ciro Podany, age 13*

ODE TO BLUE CALCITE

Born in Mexico, emigrated
Thrust into unfamiliar hands
Jagged edges, weathered
But unequaled in brilliance
Shades of blue, clear
Like the eyes of a wise man
Many faces on one, facades
Hiding its true nature
Frozen inside, iceberg
Cold to the touch
Isolated from the world, lonely
Dark blue surrounded by unyielding ice
Encased in white, untouchable
Wanting to escape
Icy temper, emotionless
Like the grim rain
Male, estranged son
Flooding of memories
Winter brewing, December
Sky before a storm

~ *Connie Zhang, age 14*

FAMILY

Pandas are my nature
Chinese, warm and soft
Minorities in the forest
Of birds, tigers, deer.

The moon in full bloom
Full moon festival
Towering with light
Celebrated through mooncakes
Cut in half
Sweet brown dough
Around a golden yellow yolk
Like the sun on the horizon.

Juicy smells from the house full
     of people
Sardines packed in cans
On Chinese New Year's Eve
Small red envelopes bringing
     good luck.

Chopped square tofu: Mah-Jongg tiles,
Characters of peace and happiness on
     the walls
House washed
Sand by the shore to clean away
Bad memories of the old year.

Fierce, respected dragons, beautiful
     Venerable phoenixes
Mystical authorities of the past
Grandmothers and Grandfathers
Who will look after us in the future.

Children of the new: flowers still in
     bloom
Hear the familiar sounds of the language
Yellow chopsticks dabbing everywhere
Bamboos in the forest.

~ *Phoebe Tang, age 14*

MY FAMILY HAS PRIDE
Tina Nagai, age 8

The buttery sun rays
tickle the left-over platters of
last night's
heaping dew.
Leaves
washed clean of their troubles
lay beaten and crippled
trampled by November's soggy shoes.

~ *Shallin Ris, age 14*

TREE

At the leaf
My brother is building his Lego helicopter
He fights in World War I
A collision, and the colors fall apart
The tiles spill to the floor and scatter
Apart like the rest

At the branch
My father is reading the Chinese newspaper on the Internet
He clicks the mouse like a champion athlete
Many pages flash across the screen
Green, purple, red, blue, black, yellow
Yet he understands the colors of rainbow

At the stem
My mother is heaving a white mop
Up and down, up and down the olive staircase
The carpet is sagging with the moisture
But my mother still scrubs endlessly
At the black spot near the third stair

At the root
My grandmother bustles in her kitchen
Ferociously grinding beans in her soybean machine
The milky foam leaks and splatters the table in little puddles
And stains her purple jacket
But she is too busy attacking the broken buttons

~ *Nancy Xu, age 14*

AUGUST

The drying sunflowers in the vase,
the flies lazing around the fan,
the hay bales being brought into the barn.
Grandma's apple pies filling the house.
Men in the golden fields call to each other.
A dog barks lazily,
awakened from his nap as a chestnut horse
trots by.

End of August.
My sister brings water,
cool and sweet, like a new spring
into the white farmhouse.
Vegetables in the cool brown earth
ready to rise from it.
Cow tails swish pesky flies away.
The hot tin roof glints in the sunlight.

The tall hay bales wait.
I climb to the top and look at the sky.
The lazy sun winks down at me.
I feel so small—
a pin in the hay bale, impossible to find.

~ *Tyler Lehman, age 15*

POSEIDON IN THE INFIRMARY

Cold water
lying still between cement walls—
a river once, I guess,
but now you barely move
content to sleep
in peace and silence.
Your watery eyes
once so clear and blue
have fogged now,
grown brown,
clouded with dirt and algae
and your skin is covered with wrinkles—
ripples—
lazy in the breeze.

In your youth you were
a river
an ocean
a thunderstorm—
you were Poseidon.
But lying here now,
in the gray concrete bunker,
you are dying.
Old and infirm, the strength you had
to rush, to fall, to crush
is gone
and you are left with age
and the wet wool smell
of dead water.

~ *Anaïs Koivisto, age 15*

67

RETURN

Bring me home by moonlit path
where pale moon stains the ochre earth.
Tell me where to go.
Away from the place where the yellow lanterns glow
Where the insects gather for heat
in the lonely night.
Surround me with trees
where the stubborn houses refuse
to stand
Where the rain breaks delicately
against green leaves.
Take me to the place
where the stars do not hide timidly
ashamed of their beauty
Where the smells that rise from the earth
guide me.
Guide me home to the forest
where I can find myself again
hidden in the leaves.

~ *Celia La Luz, age 15*

I have used up all
of my river.
Nothing is left but the stones.

~ *Oona Lyons, age 16*

RIVER OF MEMORIES

Alpenglow bright
red over the Russian
River kids at play

Salmon
leaping suddenly
I'm back in

Benares people
are shouting
bargaining people

Everywhere cleaning
the polluted river
transported back

In time to my childhood gurgling
tormented brown
river calling me for help

Too young to
understand the cry, I
smile unaware of water's plight

Back in California, almost
a man, I
smile and kids splash

Bend down and scoop
floating Styrofoam
box from swirling

Smile transforms to
a determined
gaze.

~ *Daniel William Seeman, age 16*

DON'T CUT THE BRANCH YOU'RE SITTING ON
Valeriy Polushkin, age 12

PAST CREST AND SWELL

The pulse, the beat of waves
On rocks on sand
Pulsing over me and over
Dissolving me
They sweep me carelessly out
Past crest and swell
To the curved world stretched by a naked hand
Holding me delicately at the nape of my neck
Expanding and expounding—this is how it should feel
My heart thrust open to two reverberating, continual
Circles of sky and water
Merging
And forming my own shell out of fragments of stars
Broken, sewn then mended
The sea traces the seams of my face
Like no one else can, draws my breath
From me and into the deep
Healing sea-foam green
Pours through my skin and streams out of my fingertips
The sea deposits me gagging salt water on the shore
Separate again.

~ *Kiya Gornik, age 17*

CIRCLES

I dream in circles
if I dream at all.
He walks in my sleep,
I watch his footsteps fall;
when darkness ends, it is the
     end of all.

I dream in shadows,
soft and undefined
the glows and candle-flickers
of my mind;
he walks through places I will
     never find.

I dream in rhythms,
in movements, startled motions,
the toss and roll and tumbled
     foam of oceans;
he laughs at my impressions.

His silences surround me
     and I drown.
I speak his smiles, his whispers
     drag me down;
there is so little I can call my own.
My dreams are always him.
I do not dream,
I want to sink, and sinking,
     want to swim.

I do not close my eyes till I am
     tired.
If night was made for sleep,
     then why the moon?

I wake from dreams
still dreaming I'm awake;
my candle has burned out,
a blackened wick.
I wake in circles
if I wake at all.

~ Anaïs Koivisto, age 17

INVITATION

Now I want only for you to dance with me.
Let's slip off our summer shoes, black with dust,
and stand in the froth, you—scared of this new
muddy rhythm, me—pulling you in.
You would budge, shifting off the bank, making us
four sun-blessed ankles in the cold water.
You'd have to listen to keep up with me,
to stay in time with the improvising shore.
Don't look mad as wavelets tease at the pant leg
rolled thick over your knees.
Why not, instead, watch and hear the water
sing ungrammatically into the arms of the bay?
Notice it leads the willing fog,
open your hand and lean in.

But I know you, with your star charts
and telescope. You mean to stand in the sky.

Dance with me anyway. Feel giddy
knees weaken. And while we grow planted
in the mud and your sun starts to dim,
melting into the water far away,
see your night sky tug at the darkening swells
until the heavens are liquid and Orion
breaks and its tadpole stars swim,
lighting the eyes of carp that brush our feet.
This is where things are whole, the nexus.
Dancing, sprouting fins and wings,
you would be knee-deep in the dream.

~ *Valerie Madamba, age 17*

FISHING

Cold this evening—
I'll blame the river.
Gazing on these stars
affords me some respite;
a cost-effective nepenthe.
Stuck between the act:
to
fish
or
bite?
It's rough when you're the angler and the angled.

But, so it goes;
at once sedated, absorbed and secreted.
I am taken unawares
by this cricket,
whose chirping is cavernously
splendid tonight.

~ *Mercury Ellis, age 17*

FIRST WINTER'S FOG

The fog floats upon the fields
Blanketing each hay bale, barn, animal—
Shrouding every object in its icy, cobwebbing
Mist,
The moon reflects upon the stilled waters
Of the slough, shining as bright
As in the sky, glowing with the stillness
Of the night.
Trees, bare from winter's cold,
Stand alone, silhouetted against the sky
Of evening, reaching, gesturing as the breeze stirs
Their freezing branches.
"On the night that you were born," Mom says,
"There was fog."
"Fog," you think,
"Fog."

~ *Margit Bowler, age 10*

ON THE SHORES OF
GOOSE LAKE

Bronzed
By last summer's breath
Last golden leaf
Drifts to your feet
Calling
Go now.

Scales bright
Against the night sky of river
Last shining salmon
Fights the icy water
Urging
You must fly.

Last sun ray
Caressing your feathers
Fades away
Uttering
Follow me.

Last chipmunk
Cheeks bulging
Walnuts and berries
Chirping
Hurry! Take wing!

First icicle
Frosty ornament
Adorns the bare, sleeping maple
Whispering
Farewell geese.

~

Madeline Wong, age 11

I ASKED

I asked the sky why it was blue
And it smiled and blew out clouds of white
I asked the night why it was dark
And it reached out to me and sprinkled lights
        across the sky
I asked the sun why it was there
And it cried and set and the moon rose
I asked the tree to bloom
And it twisted and the blossoms burst
I asked the wind to blow
And it did and the flowers were blown away
I asked the plants why they grew
And they whispered and wilted
I asked myself what was wrong
And the sky darkened
The stars dulled
The wind blew
And I kept quiet
And everything was perfect.

~ *Khatsini Simani, age 11*

REFLECTIONS

Sometimes,
when the mountains
reflect on rivers,
you can find out things
you never knew before.
There are flowers up there,
rocks like clouds,
a little snow becomes a creek
and grows into a river.

~

Lindsay Ryder, age 11

THE LATE ROSE

It curls by the gate, biding its time.
Spring is gone, and Summer is waning.
Autumn? A hairsbreadth away.

The breeze sweeps on,
Swinging the gate on its rusty hinges,
Gently filtering through the sun-hued bud.

Creamy pink deep within,
Petals the color of the sunset sky,
Tinged with gold.

My eyes trace the path of your
Slender stalk, saw-edged leaves
Whispering quietly to Zephyrus.

The last fresh petal unfolds,
The silk-smooth skin of secret treasures
Spilling perfume into the woods.

Four days of full-fledged glory,
The moaning wind
Spills your beauty on the soil.

As crimson leaves crunch.

I tread softly, knowing
That you will have another year to rest,
And I will have another year to wait.

~

Jane S. Jiang, age 11

BEFORE A SNOWFALL

A late autumn leaf falls and drifts to the floor
brushed by the cold breeze

the grass
takes its last look at the world above

a lone crow
silhouetted against the blank sky

~

Becky Davis, age 11

PICTURE THIS

A babbling brook snaking its way through damp Seattle
neighborhoods
And on its banks, vicious blackberries
Lurking behind every bend, ready to take the stream over,
Like a pack of snarling wolves

Imagine the maples
Each one giving its all to touch the sky.
One maple's adventure fails,
Its last leaf flutters to the ground

A fork in the stream,
Break off the trail and travel to another place and time

Hear
The robin's call, mumble of water over the rocks

See the salmon
Every scale glistening in the morning sun

Stop here.

~

Luke Hussey, age 11

RIVER OF WORDS

As we have our words, so does the river
Drip, drop
It always has something to say
Trickle, tinkle
A cat can never get its tongue, even as it falls
Whoosh, sploosh
Even in a deep freeze, it will still talk
Creak, crack
Listen child, if you listen hard
You will hear its life story,
From melting
Drip, drop
To flowing
Trickle, tinkle
To diving
Whoosh, sploosh
Then to frozen
Creak, crack
Take a little time to hear what
It has to say
Drip, drop
Trickle, tinkle
Whoosh, sploosh
Creak, crack
Listen to the river as it always
Has something to say.

~ *Nygil Milligan, age 11*

All summer long they come—
with or without dogs,
in loose, slow-moving bunches or alone,
hiking the steep, narrow path past the blackberries,
past the stream that is little more than a trickle now
in the hot depths of summer.

In the winter the stream swells—a vein, a pulsing artery of water
for deer that trip down from the forest's edge,
for raccoons that hide by daylight beneath our deck.
Chickadees, nuthatches, pine siskins
fly in and out of low, brambly willows that line the banks.

The stream dips beneath the surface,
through pipes, culverts, under streets
and out again, into the wan winter sun,
a quarter of a mile away where it joins the slough,
brown floodwaters mingling.

Past ash and cottonwood,
in and out of cattails, willows,
past the place where each year
a family of ducks return
faithful to the stream,
and the huge blue heron is sometimes seen.

Moving toward the river,
where geese honk overhead,
and finally to its end
in the marshy reservoir,
the tiny stream which began
across our street
has traveled eighteen long miles
and now mingles with other waters,
glistening in the sun.

~

Aaron Wells, age 12

PEACEFUL LAKE

Bright moon
Dancing
On a still lake,
Gentle waves
Lapping
At the footprints
We left behind,
Our feet sinking
In soft sand,
Our silhouettes
Standing alone
On a peaceful water.

~ *Tori Borish, age 12*

COMING BACK TO SKYKOMISH

Cabin in the country
High on the hill
Overlooking the river

River rushes
Drops of compelling power

Keep on swimming, salmon

Proud mountain
Like a pointing finger
Snow melting in the sun

Forest awaits
Calling to the world
Trees two thousand strong

Sweet apple tree beckons
Gnarled branches outstretched
Calling, *Come Back*
Come Back,
This is the World.

~ *Kate Lund, age 12*

TWO WORLDS

golden rays fan out
across the horizon

dewdrops tickle
the blazing meadows

birds gossip
in the lofty cherry trees

blooming flowers
praise upwards

but what is this?

ah, you are like me, little one.

a cocoon
tingling with excitement to escape   yet
we cannot leave home so soon.

~ *Estee Ward, age 12*

RIVER OF WORDS

Angelina Ooi Wei Wei, age 11

DEAR STARS,

Please come down to me—
I cannot live on
Mist and moonshine
Alone
I meander, past
Cambered willows—they weep
And trail their
Haggard branches as the
Doves, lighting on an arching limb
Coo a low
Tremulous song, and a single note
Hangs in the air. But so ephemeral
Are these scintillas of
Joy. The very
Air itself is
Melancholy
Winds whisper a
Soft contralto to my
Plangent song. This is
Why I call to you, eternally
Luminescent stars—
For your company
I am willing
To wait.

~ *Jane S. Jiang, age 13*

GLOW

The morning's first glow
Smothered the horizon,
Rays pouring over the clouds
Spilling into the ocean,
Crawling across the sea
Calling for me
And I took it.

Rays and all
I stuffed the light
In my pocket
Next to the moon, stars
Stolen from beneath their black quilt
Points askew
Stabbing through the worn seams
Of my jeans.

Marvelous melodies
Symphonies beyond comprehension
Nature's chords
Suspended in nothingness
Wisely woven within
The willows
Quick within the roots
That nourish my soul.

~ *Khatsini Simani, age 13*

INNER SPACE

where thoughts roam grasslands
dreams spring like graceful gazelle evading hunger ravaged fear
ideas the bee-eaters, finches, sunbirds, kingfishers
delicate feathers sporting blues, greens, purple, red
shade and hue ignored, pure color
brown, gray, mix and meld with earth
—its dry sticks
swift, gone like that, another meal another marula tree
another back of an elephant
the subconscious, influential
a slow-moving mold of being
stable flat feet kick up brush, clear the way

a reflection of self in a serenely deep blue
where waves hug the shore tight
along the inlets and points of mind
sand and sea's convocation
the shallows, whose turquoise glow shelters corals
threatened, easily weakened and corrupted
twisted and shattered
a code
moral

where truth is found like glowworms under stones
where purpose lies in high, curvy branches

~ *Dezmond Goff, age 14*

CHANGING SEASONS

fiery orange leaves litter the sidewalk
while a misty haze dances over the field
a faded American flag droops
left out since 4th of July
a lawn chair rests under the shade of a maple tree
and a lonely RV waits
now that fall has settled in

~ *Ellie Crutcher, age 14*

HORIZON PLEASE CONTINUE

Until the end of the sky
Your
Mingled tinted twilights
Prelude to a pearly sliced moon
You are
the dividing line
between gravity and geese
Crossed by dimmed silhouettes

~ *Ginny Drake, age 14*

THE DESCHUTES RIVER

The traveler Deschutes
Meanders her way through gossiping aspen groves,
Tiptoes through old-growth cathedrals,
And waits impatiently in the traffic jams of estuaries.

The lioness Deschutes
Tears at mud banks,
Crushes rocks,
And rampages out of her bed to curl her grip around land.

The thunderbird Deschutes
Flies over waterfalls,
Rumbles over rapids,
And paints the sky with summer clouds.

The queen Deschutes
Presides over meadows,
Reigns over leafy subjects,
And wears a silver crown of foam and bubbles.

The mother Deschutes
Shelters crying fish,
Plays with cheeky otters,
And comforts the lonely trees.

My friend the Deschutes
Performs a ballet every Tuesday and Saturday night,
Tells me secrets, knows all mine,
And lets me write poetry about her.

~ *Kelly Cox, age 15*

WADING STREAM

I typed in *watersheds* and the keys
gave back, in four-color
maps with rivulets—
the thin veining of lives written
shorthand, the ink for blood.

But pixel maps do not imagine—cannot dream
like I have, of moon-gilt streams come
down for wading-nights, and stars
and wind-gust songs amongst the living trees.

Tonight we wait, blind
in the veil of dart and maples
we peer between
the leaves—but hush!
        —a dream comes wading. There, down by
that rippled moon—do you see?
 . . . hold still, don't
breathe.

~ *Jane S. Jiang, age 16*

GRASSHOPPER

Had one
Kept it
Tickling
It jumped away
I let it go
I was touching
Something live

CHAPULÍN

Tenía uno
Lo guardé
Me hacía cosquillas
Salió en un salto
Lo dejé
Yo estaba tocando
Algo vivo

~ *Oscar Trejo Renteria, age 7*

I LOVE MY DOG

The summer sun danced off the water
While I played in the S-shaped bend
In the East River.
I stomped in the water
With my puddle boots
And watched my dog Taylor flop down
Like a child flops down on her bed.
She looked like a lump of angel rock
Protecting me as I
Plomped,
Plomped,
Plomped
In the shallow edge
Of the river.
I was always the happiest
Kid in the world
Playing with my dog
In the sun
At the S-shaped bend
In the East River.

~ *Avery Forsythe, age 8*

TALKING TREES

Trees talk
All the time
They yell
They whisper
They even rhyme
When they're mad
They blow their leaves
Sometimes they let out a deep s-i-g-h
They tell the truth
They even lie.

~ *Erin Kopal, age 11*

LIGHT

Outside
Is all filled up with snow.
It is magic powder;
It has a quiet, silent glow.
Feathers from the sky create
Soft pillows on the ground.
Summer is much louder.

~ *Annie Ochs, age 11*

IS THERE A PLACE TO REST MY SOUL?

As snowflake stars fall through my scars;
As dusk grows restless and valleys get wide;
Winds get heavy and souls go hard, living through nightmares.
Is there love, is there hope
Is there light in this unraveling loophole?

~ *Crystal Schwaigert, age 12*

ROOFLESSNESS

Then I'll just sit right down—
here in this little stone fortress
sunken into the red-dry hillside,
so that all I see of that city
will be the tops of skyscrapers
and just a bit of chain-link.

I'm not scared.
I have a green laminated name tag,
PARKER,
to remind myself who I am.

With Lone Peak and Olympus
fading to white blue on the horizon,
I'm slow to notice

the green-gray sages
and dormant scrub oak
forming low walls all around me.
And I wonder if I really
should have brought my boot prints
(and butt print)
onto the snow rug of this hollow.
In past evenings
the creatures may have gathered here
to consider a retreat for the day
they knew would come,
when the city crept eastward
to fill the northern canyons
with little skyscrapers.

~ *Parker Shaw, age 15*

105

COYOTE

Run
They are coming
with their loud machines
       their concrete
       their egos
Run Coyote
over the foothills
and up the steep terrain
to the wilderness
to the deep snow

       Stop
take one last look
mark your territory
Perhaps they will listen
Leave your scattered tracks
your signature
       This is yours
       Sign your name

~ *Corinne Neves, age 16*

{ CREATURE STORY }
Mira Darham, age 9

106

MOONLIGHT RISING

Coyote,
there's nothing to feed your lean body,
so you run away,
shyly, quickly.
Don't look to either side, just run,
leaving your story behind you. . . .

As the moon crests,
the jackrabbit wiggles out from
a blanket of snow.
Hop, hop . . . no, that doesn't taste good,
move on to better things.
Stop.
Something is there, watching you.
Knowing that you are dinner,
muscles tense and you burst into flight,
your skidded footprints showing us your safety.

The sunlight begins to crawl.
Small mouse jumps out from under a foundation
and bounces in the snow. Hmm . . .
Nothing. Just the overwhelming pressure of silence.

You are being watched by trees and rocks
and mountains and God
in every crystal snowflake.

We know where you have been,
waiting for the moon to rise and dance
in the eerie blue world.

But we will find you,
in each sentence of your journey
left in poetry,
impressed in snow.

~

Alexandra Rich, age 16

THE WIND AND I

I find, Somewhere
East . . .
Of the Midwest bohemia
where the mountains hide digested by the scrub oak
into winter crystals knee-deep and dying
to roll with the wind and its flute music, its voice.

Listen, Quiet . . .
It hides in the trees, in the fish-bone branches,
drips in amber sap, and softly screams
for the last forest breath before there's
nowhere else to sing . . .

Yet it flies!
Hit the mountain, the water,
curve under its crystal cliffs of white,
run the pine and the maple.
Carve life into the sculpture with wind song!
Soar the high places through hawk's feathers.
Dive . . .
for food into running rabbit
long legged across the field,
faster

up through deer legs beating the snow
to the rhythm of the song
and curve down through coyote's heartbeat
giving chase
quickly,
then disappearing
into the quaking aspen
and flying on into forever.

Listen,
Quiet . . .
Let the wind shape you.

~ *John Kinnear, age 17*

IMPRINTS IN THE SNOW

Footprints parade across
meadows of powdered paper
painting them with animal versions
of hieroglyphics,
foreign languages taught
within walls
created by the Oquirrh
and Wasatch Mountains,
using their stride and straddle
as pens to share,
through this written language,
their experiences and dreams.

Here I stand among countless stories
seeing nothing
and thinking
I understand everything.

~ *Amy Allred, age 17*

POINT OF ORDER

I am curled around wood
and air

I touch my fingers, but
they are numb

It's too bad
there are no
fireflies in Utah
when I sleep on my
hat in February

I don't really care what anyone
says about the trees

~ *Zachary England, age 17*

112

DREAMING TREES

I never liked to live in nature
Sit with my feet burrowed in the sand
The guided tour of God's Labyrinth
Seemed like nothing more than a frosted cave
Where dreams were lost
But then
A dragonfly hovered and teased
Above my eyes
As the sun hit the Wasatch Mountains.
And I realized
That it is everywhere
That each new day it is reborn
When I shake the sleep out of my hair
The earth's breath absorbs my nighttimes
And takes it to the trees
Suddenly
Give and take seems so sincere
And courtesy unfolds
As my sleepy dreams are
Absorbed by the trees.

~ *Amanda Gaither, age 17*

NATURAL SELECTION OR:
HOW DAN MCLANE WAS NEARLY LOST FOREVER

We were standing on the hill
knee-deep in snow
(the powdery kind that gets
in your ear when you fall down
and you don't notice it's there
until it melts
and there's water running
down the side of your face)
So anyway there we were
standing knee-deep in snow
at Red Butte Gardens
supposedly taking field notes and
Dan said, right there in the open, standing at the edge of the hill
he said, "I'm the king of this mountain!" and that's when
the ground dropped out
from under him
and he was gone
hands in his pockets
cascading down the mountain
sending up sprays
of crystal-cold snow
his tumbling body

silhouetted
against the white ground
against the white mountains
against the white sky
until he got caught in some scrub oak
halfway down the mountain
halfway to the river
caught in some scrub oak
which Nick and I thought was hilarious
because he wasn't the king of the mountain at all.

~ *Tim Wirkus, age 18*

THE RIVER

Ducks swim under the bridge,
playing tag
Squirrel peeks at me,
runs away
Deer tracks in dry mud
Grasses bent in a soft, secret bed.

~

Rokendy Johnson, age 7

{ **LITTLE DUCKLING** }
John Kwok, age 17

WISHING DUST

The rain, the trees
the road and my heart
are part of the world.

The windy moonlight
and sunlight
are like wishing dust
that is coming down
on me.

~ *Tyler Mitchell, age 8*

BUGNIBBLE

Wind blows,
Leaves fall.
Dead leaves hit the ground.
Bugs nibble holes
In the leaf's rattling carpet.

~ *Calvin Hargis, age 8*

THE ANIMAS RIVER

The river flows like
cursive writing, calmly. The sun
shines on the water
like fire.
The wind whistles
my writing—*s, c, e*
loop into my notebook,
as the river loops
through the trees.

~ *Casey Perkins, age 9*

CROSSING EL DESIERTO

When you cross the *frontera* you
go with *sed y calor,* you feel
happy *porque* you
are going *con un compañero*
But at the same
time *tu te sientes triste* because
you and him are illegals.

They were walking through
el norte but as they walked
they saw a cactus, green like a lime
they saw a man
and they asked him *por aqua*
but he *no los escuchaba*
because he was running
and he was old.
They started to walk again
with no *comida.*
Una amiga se cayó y su companero
was still walking *tan rápido.*
She saw a *tuna en el nopal*
and she cut it *con sus dientes.*
El sol estaba muy caliente como una quemazón.

Walking again *pero ella sola,*
she stopped because it was *noche*
se perdió. It was hard to sleep
because the *noche estaba muy fría.*
She *sonió que* she was in *el río* drinking *agua*
y cuando se despertó she was
in the same place.

No one was there, *estaba sola*
no one came
except the moon, and in the light
she could see *su compañero*
walking toward her.

~ *Diana Ortiz, age 11*

121

IN THE GLITTERING WORLD

In the glittering world
Water is magic, mystery
Called down by the Zuni Bow Priest
With his headdress of clouds
Or danced into being
By the people of the Pueblo
Their arms arcing into rainbows
Flash of fire and thunder
Silver beads shoot through the swollen clouds
Wounding peccary, she flees
As the torrent thunders through the arroyo
Carving the land into salt and silt and sand
Ground squirrel darts through the shimmering spray
As the waters spill over his burrow
It is the baptism of the desert
Healing the cracked clay
The Canyon People know
The universe spirals, intertwined
Dark and light, river and mountain
The same water was here when the earth began.

~ *Todd Detter, age 13*

⟩ MORNING SCENE IN MY HOMETOWN ⟨
Jeane Renee T. Nubla, age 14

IN THE WEST

In the West, water flows uphill
Leaping across the Tehachapi Mountains
To fill the mouth of the City of Angels.
In the West, the streams serve us
Captured and prisoned, in tunnels, in siphons and aqueducts
Bleeding into our irrigated lands.
In the West, once the rivers' voices
Coaxed the salmon surging thick against the current,
Lured the antelope and bison herds to their banks.
Now there is silence.
In the West, the rivers are the Disappeared
Their bones buried in a common grave
We forget their names
And call the land "Desolation."

~ *Todd Detter, age 14*

BRANDING IN THE SPRING

As the grass begins to green
And the calves begin to grow
A big job lies ahead of us
Past all the winter snow.

The calves are later separated
After an early start
As we began to sort them through
And break their mothers' hearts.

They're later forced into a chute
By my aggressive dog
And one by one they go through
And face the iron rod.

The smell of burnt hair
Rises in the sky
As they're marked with our hot iron
Clank! The gate swings open and out the young calves fly.

~

Annie Johnson, age 14

VIRGA

Sky stretched tight
over hard dry land
The rivers are ribbons of silky dust
snaking arroyos
tangled lengths of abandoned beds
where rocks cannot be smoothed
by the smooth steady rush

Clouds pass hurriedly by
refusing the smallest breath of moisture
bearing their gifts elsewhere
while the sun returns to beat down
upon a landscape it has thoroughly tamed
Wind whistles through, sparkling
as freshness is borne to regions afar

Now it is an afternoon in August
the sky a palette of unreal blues and grays
Clouds here for a short stay only
tear suddenly open at their swollen seams
and the rain begins to fall
It evaporates briskly above the horizon
but soon violent drops raise the sulky dust

Narrow canyon beds rush swollen with water
pounding forward like the sound of blood in your ears
exuberantly destructive for a few short moments
before the sun shreds the velvet clouds
before the earth sucks the damp greedily away
The sky gazes blankly, inexpressive
and the desert settles in to wait

~ *Mallory A. Jensen, age 16*

WATER BABIES

La Llorona thrust her children
Into the river's mouth
And watched it swallow them
Like silver minnows.

Gleaming flies buzzed on the bus.
Gasoline fumes floated, thin clouds over our heads.
Juan and I shared an orange while *Abuelo* whispered,
In the USA we would eat ice cream every day.

Trudging through dense desert dusk,
We breathed the scent of green mesquite.
Staring up at dark jagged mountains, down at tracks of tire sandals
Mama stumbled on a cattle guard.
Wrapped in her *rebozo,* the baby woke and whimpered.
Coyote Man whirled, hissing curses.

We reached the brown bubbling *mole* of the river.
Our boats were plywood, laid over tubes.
The Coyote snatched the child from her arms.
The weight of two would make it sink, he snarled.
Only a moment while he didn't watch
For the current to catch the fragile ship, carrying it away.

Mama didn't scream or speak at all
As they pulled her from the shallows.
Look, they cried, pointing to Juan and me,
You have beautiful children still.
While her empty eyes sank into the swirling water
They led her away and the Coyote told my father,
I will not charge you for that child although the tube was lost.

La Llorona weeps for her children
As they sink like stones.
Or do they float and twirl like trout
Living on mist and damselflies
In the circles of the river?

~ *Todd Detter, age 17*

WORSHIP

All my life I have been looking for the one that has the wisdom of the
     world all in her liquid hands—
the one that has seen generations of humans come and go like the seasons,
the one that has seen the history of the world and its excruciating pain.
She moves through borders and cultures, seeing the beauty of every
     person's soul and spirit.
She holds our lives in the ripples of her body.
The one that carries a world of swimming spirits in the innermost part
     of her belly.
She is the destroyer, the source of life, the past, present, and future.
She is the giver who never stops giving as we destroy and pollute her soul,
the one that transforms herself into sparkling white snow and crystals
     of ice.
The one that flows through deserts, mountains, and rain forests,
creating gods everywhere she goes.
She is everything; she is water.

~ *Lesther Lopez, age 16*

UNTITLED
Bahareh Talakoob, age 15

THE SNAKE

The snake lives in water.
The snake swims with its tail.
It sings a song to itself.

~

Robert Farr, age 6

THE RAIN

Dark
Pouring
Scary
Black
Puddle
Night

~

Maddison Boewe, age 6

THE SCIOTO RIVER

Icy cold water
Wet as can be
Moving very fast like me.

~

Radhika Patel, age 7

A crystal
snowflake
falls down
on the
freezing
white
floor
of
January.

~ *Martha Bregin, age 7*

SEASONS IN OUR WATERSHED

Four short seasons come and go,
Filled with sunshine, sleet and snow,
First is Spring and then Summer and Fall,
With Winter being last of all,
Each is special in its own way,
Having its own unique bouquet.

A robin marks the start of Spring,
Happily singing to everything,
Then the blossoms begin to bud,
Slowly grass conceals the mud,
The swirling river will overflow,
And green grass will start to grow.

Then comes Summer, hot and dry,
Until dark rain clouds fill the sky,
It's time to swim and play and run,
And to tan yourself in the hot, hot sun,
You can fish in the river and climb up some trees,
Or sit in a meadow surrounded by bees.

Next comes Fall with beauty and sound,
Colorful leaves blanket the ground,
The air smells strongly of soft, damp leaves
A chilly Fall wind, the earth receives,
Squirrels sit in trees and chatter and scold,
Then comes a frost, the beginning of cold.

Next comes the snowflakes, so perfect to see,
This is the time to sled and to ski,
The river is silent and shiny and slick,
But you won't break through, if the ice is thick,
Cardinals are back with their fiery red,
And the chickadee with the black cap on his head.
When Winter is finally at its end,
The whole cycle starts over again.

~

Rebecca Davison, age 12

LUCKY

Osprey swoops downward
Brook trout leaps skyward, airborne—
Lucky day, for one

~

Clay McMullen, age 11

GOLDFISH

Clear flowing
   Water
      Rushes down
         Stream
           As tiny
              Glazing
           Goldfish scatter
     To
    Their mother
  Like
Lightning.

~ *Stefani Galik, age 8*

RICHES OF THE RIVER
Maxine Ty, age 13

BLACK HOLE DIARY

I am royal purple,
a reigning river of capability.
I used to be an
elephant sigh
until crisp stars
poked their passion into my raspy laugh.
I am the space between fingers,
fragile, empty,
veined, pulsing,
smooth & crinkled.
At times I remember the word folded in my heart:
closure.
I have let go of my name:
Night Sky.

~ *Abbey Tadros, age 13*

THE FOREST'S HAIKU

Walking the deer path
Milkweed seeds catch in my hair
Eight quail in bramble.

~

Ben Santos, age 13

THE VOICE OF A RIVER

Thundering peace
Crashing silk
The whispering ripples
Of a pounding melody

Flying spirit
Treasure stored
The shadows deep as forever
A shimmering glance

At what might have been
What could still be
The river
Knows no time

Carrying secrets
Through forever
Never stopping, unchanging
Power

Tugging memories
From a crystal reflection
A silent voice
Shouting to the soul

~ *Sarah Beth Comfort, age 13*

HISTORY OF A CORNFIELD

pale winter
a barren field with broken stalks
wilted, a faded cream—
like whey and curds strained from milk

budding spring
the cool breeze whispers over the dead field
bringing it back to life
and upon it a soft green carpet of leaves spreads

thirsty summer
rain rushes from the saturated clouds
and flows into the sun-parched ground

in the porous ground the roots of the corn plants
soak up the water,
quenching their thirst

and as the leaves grow greener
the kernelled bounty slowly forms

harvest fall
the sun shines over the golden leaves
as the corn is gathered
the leaves dance their final waltz

twilight casts a curtain over the last act of the play
and the dawn signals its beginning again

~ *Priyanka Bose, age 14*

RIVER SENSES

The river is a sheet on a clothesline
Rippling when the wind strokes it.
Sandbars: half-submerged, lazy turtles
Warm in the sun
Yet refreshed by the swirling deep.
Leafy towers arch their backs,
Sway long, brown arms
In the direction of the seeping cool.
Squishy algae clots discarded bones of giant creatures.
In years agone they knelt for sips of sweetness
To moisten parched throats.
Graceful herons stalk flashing minnows,
Who weave in and out, always ahead,
Taunting the great gray birds.
After minutes of useless precision
The herons soar to the above
Leaving only delicate marks
Where their twig-like toes brushed the sand.
Fairy breezes slither snake fingers through sparkling sand,
Billow out above the rapids,
And sink down to the slender golden grasses
Where bowing blades murmur.

The wind flails wild arms.
Prairies swirl in a mad frenzy of waves
Until the wind tires of its wild play.
Dancing breezes pirouette towards serene river pools
Circling back from whence they came.
The wind, heaving a heavy sigh,
Drifts downward.
It collapses on water,
Allowing its fury to be lulled
By the rocking sapphire beneath.

~ *Irene Beeman, age 14*

AN ENDLESS RHYTHM

Waves play a smooth song
Inky water under a full moon
A surface that shimmers
Slight waves disturb
the glassy surface
The water sighs
Never changes its rhythm
Pulls in and out
Always on time
Silence, even the gulls sleep
Only dreaming stars,
a sleepy moon,
and restless waves accompany me
My troubles pass away
Pulled into the endless sighs
Melt into the marred surface
of the water
There is nowhere else
I would rather be

~ *Devan Allard, age 15*

DAVIDSON CREEK

I was born in the
belly of that river.

    Again and again
      I go there

       to catch bullfrogs
       to lie flat on the wet
bank
          to let the brown snake
           slither past
       to find the meaning of life
         and lose it

to build my soul
    of rushes

      to paint your face
in the riverbed

     and go home
       dreaming of its
         voice.

~ *Elizabeth Clark, age 17*

PULLING LIFE ONWARD

Come, my cousins said.
The moon is out on the lake, come see.
And so, in pajamas,
we padded along the boardwalk,
our footsteps soft and dull on old timbers.
But never a creak, never the gentle lap of water.
All was stillness, blackness,
no hint of the waving green that draped my paddle
when I guided my canoe in daylight, exploring, wandering
into the lilied coves of the island.
All was marbled darkness, marbled moonlight.
I never saw a lake so deep
with stars, as if a step could drop us
into lasting silence.
Life seemed to sleep. And yet,
between the weathered railings, moonlight
touched spiders weaving in the darkness,
long legs industrious
without a ray of sun.

In the reeds beside us, something
waddled and rustled and chewed,
and when I leaned over, a muskrat
vanished with a hollow splash.
Then all seemed lifeless again
until, with a click, my cousin's flashlight
put out the stars, rendered the water transparent,
and there, on the sandy bottom,
a snapping turtle roamed
from clump to clump of weeds, from mouthful to mouthful,
pulling life onward, always onward,
till we flipped off the light and he faded once more
into a depth of stars.

~ *Ann Pedtke, age 17*

BELTING BROADWAY

The wind whips my face
as the boat accelerates.
I let it flip and toss my hair
as my feet dangle over the edge.
White foam tickles my toes.

The sun pours down
across the green and blue waves,
each rough bump
now lined with glittering gold.

My friend sits next to me,
and when the first notes of a song
        escape her lips,
I join in,
the wind stealing the lyrics
as soon as they slip from my mouth.

I smile when the last note
hangs in the air.
My voice is weak from roaring
        the words,
but I fall back and laugh with
        Amelia.
Again?

I nod.
I want this afternoon,
this boat ride,
this song,
this moment with Amelia
to last forever.

~ *Sarah Jordan, age 12*

RAINY DAY
You Na Park, age 15

FLAGS

Flags dot the houses
I stroll past.
Even ours is up,
a fluttering red, white and blue
against the cream-colored house.

I glance up, and for a moment I see
a patch of maple leaves
against the blue sky
with wisps of clouds.
Red, white, and blue.

~ *Joanna Kass, age 12*

MY TRIP TO THE HUDSON RIVER

Footprints all around—
Rabbit, deer, dog, coyote, squirrel, wild turkey—
Eyes watching all around
Fog in the distance
Rocks on the shore
Sounds of crows in the background
Smell of snow in the air
Water sits calm and quiet
Fog disappearing slowly
Buds in the tulip trees
Sound of footsteps in the snow
Shadows of the trees in the water.

~ *Devin Felter, age 12*

DEER PRINT

A soft indentation—
two toes—
marks the ground,
a blank reminder
of what has been here before me.
I try to feel amazed,
to marvel at this muddy imprint,
to feel lucky at my chance notice—
but I want to see the deer,
steam streaming from her nostrils
as she stares at me,
thin legs threatening
to give way,
small brown head
trembling in the cold.
I want to see her bound away,
her tail high in the air,
her two-toed hooves
marking the ground.

~ *Benjamin F. Williams, age 12*

BLUEBERRIES

I dash down the path
Behind our house.
The grass prickles my feet
As I gaze,
Searching for a patch
Of blueberries.
When I hit the jackpot,
I pick all the blueberries I can
As fast as I can,
And, without anyone else there to see,
I eat more than I plink-plong
Into the bowl.
The afternoon passes fast.
The crickets are beginning to chirp,
And before I know it,
The sun is starting to fade.
My day of blue is over.
My fingers stained with blueberry juice
Will have to be washed,
And my lips will have to be scrubbed.
But in my heart
The blue will last
Forever.

~ *Rachel Miller, age 13*

THROUGH THE EYES OF MORNING

The long
complicated
elements of morning
drape themselves across the dew-touched meadow
as if they are
lace
from the intricate garments of a queen
who has chosen
this moment
to blow a frosty kiss to her people through the fog—
so intensely ghost white
that if you look deep enough
you can see yourself.

And so I look.
Deep.
Hoping that if something as simple
yet intense,
as young
yet ancient,
as morning
knows who I am, maybe I will too.

But I only see the dew.
And the fog.

And who is anyone
through the distorted eyes of
morning?

~ *Anne Atwell-McLeod, age 13*

BREATHING VERMONT

Think of the mischievous nights
of a firefly summer
out in the field, grassy and sweet-smelling green.

Of the cool, rocky creek and the spiderwebbed tunnel
the groaning old stairs of a farmhouse
a leafy tree sound beneath your feet—
I would take even the salty whine of a mosquito.

Now, school-hardened, battle-weary,
I long for the sun that melts us, the lake water that washes
        us clean,
the floaty breeze that wraps us in a delicious cocoon
        of freedom:
for a satisfying, soul-renewing summer,
when I am I and you are you and everyone, everyone,
        rejoices in their newborn selves.

~ *Clarkie Hussey, age 13*

A SINGLE DROP

a
single
drop of crystal
suspended in time
for a golden moment
caught in the glinting light of
the sun a miniature rainbow
landscape of flowing colors
merging into a pool of molten
lava that glistens reflecting the
beauty of the outside world in a
minuscule looking glass that is
invaluable to the joy of
puddle-jumping
children

~

Emily Smith Gilbert, age 13

MY WOODS

the woods were alive
but silent as I searched
for mushrooms with my father.

now tracks crush memories
as yellow bulldozers roll
over the grove.

no more silence,
no new memories, only
the roar and raze of machines.

~

Wyatt Ray, age 13

{ TERRORIST }
Ali Khan, age 18

IN MEMORIAM

the deciduous nanny
governed and created order among the children who ran
in turn we made careful jewelry for her long willowy limbs
we sat on her lap pleading with her to tell us stories
about her roots
and the way things are

she always stood tall
protecting us from the snow and the rain
and everything outside that didn't delight us
even when her thick head of foliage began to thin

we cried when she disappeared
without warning without a funeral
we didn't know if she had been ill
or if she was murdered

or perhaps she decided
she'd had enough of this life
we never knew

in disbelief we turned away from her lonely remains
which seemed so cold and detached
and we remembered how she made us smile
we couldn't imagine she'd ever betray us
she was the tall upright beauty who had our love so fully
who we were sure would always be there

it all collapses finally
doesn't it?

nothing else was ever so good to dance around
no one ever understood us so well
she silently mothered all of us

that corner of our childhood world looks so empty now

~ *Alexis Kellner Becker, age 13*

WHEN I WAS SEARCHING FOR A POEM

a fox stepped out of nowhere.
His long legs stretched across the stone wall.
He paused as we stared,
both wondering where the other was going,
although it was obvious each was wandering—
lost.
I paused as we stared,
both wondering why the other was here,
on a stone wall,
although it was obvious each was
using it for direction—
lost.
He wasn't a sly fox—
at least I didn't see it in his eyes.
He was frightened.
I'd never seen a fox before.
I was frightened, too.

There.
A living poem—
a girl, a fox
connected
only by a stone wall
and a fear of the unknown.

~ *Zoe Mason, age 13*

DOGSWEETDOG

her brown
muzzle jerks up
from its limp resting spot
and lazily snaps at a fly
whirring by.

dozing
her paws twitch and her nose
trembles, whiskers quiver;
a low rumbling growl
escapes from her throat.
sweet dreams.

basking
in a puddle
of sunlight, her almond eyes,
half open, guard her milky
white bone.

prancing
on the lush lawn,
her favorite green
ball half concealed by her
        generous
pink lips.

gnawing
a rawhide dog
treat to pieces, fragments
of the tough delicacy litter
the oatmeal rug.

~ *Bailey Irving, age 14*

SEVEN HAIKU ON GOLDFISH AND WHY

I.
Why don't the fish drown!?
Incessantly they circle
the circular bowl.

II.
Quoth the painter: "I
wouldn't mind being the Ver-
million goldfish."

III.
What if a duck swooped
down and ate it up? Poor soul—
would it even mind?

IV.
All of you, drink up!
The seafaring fish don't mind;
cups are landish things.

V.
I've concluded ducks
and fish share intimacy—
as I do with plums.

VI.
Tell me, what do you
think amuses a fish? No,
no, I've tried juggling.

VII.
Now, consider the
hummingbird—flighty, fast, but
not quite so fluid.

~ *Maddy Johnson, age 14*

Inspired by:
Stan and Oliver, goldfish
Henri Matisse, Fauvistic painter
Rumi, mystic poet
Wallace Stevens, poet
Orrin Johnson, my brother

POSEIDON'S STEEDS

                              Reaching
                        the pinnacle,
                      the cusp of its
                      life. Foaming
                    forward, crashing
                  with might. Bringing
                treasures, from the
              sea's deep, or maybe
            driftwood that an artist
          would keep. A collision
        of fury, a fusion of hues.
The swirling greens, and the
        explosion of blues. Carrying
        minnows, ripping the weeds,
      charging the beach are Poseidon's steeds.

                         ~

           Allegra M. Hyde, age 14

ROADS

On my way home from work
I reach the road
that leads to our house
and I spy
my sister
and her best friend,
each in the supple beauty
of her tenth year,
ambling along the dirt shoulder.

Both swing small brown bags—
candy, I recognize—
as they walk, side by side,
heads together,
giggling,
arms rested upon
one another's small frames,
bright tanks
carefree and loose
on their shoulders.

How many times did I walk those steps?

My own little bag
looping off my fingertips,
the body of a friend
leaning close,
shimmering
as we skipped,
knees touching
the big blue sky,
hands clasped
around wildflowers
our faces lifted to the road ahead.

~ *Siobhan Anderson, age 17*

JOHNNY PUMP DOWN

We siphon off water from
the Johnny pump.
Rebelliously and
quite naturally.
For the simple
fact—
It's HOT!!!
No one
in their
right mind
gonna wait
to the
next rain drop.
Controllers
of the inner city,
water irrigation systems—
victims of
water fights,
get more,
but cops come around
yellin' bout they laws.
We close up shop
till they leave
then enjoy summer once more.

~ *David Reeves, age 17*

WISHY-WASHY WATER

Wishy-washy water
Flowing from the sink.
Wishy-washy water
Time to get a drink.
Wishy-washy water
Going down the drain.
Wishy-washy water
I hope it will rain.

~ *Thornton Blease, age 6*

THE ART OF CREEKS

When the sun sets,
the creek turns
shiny yellow,
which I paint.
When the moon
is in the sky,
the creek is shiny white,
which I paint.

Slithering water
keeps going,
keeps going.
While under
the water,
the shiny gold rocks
live.
The water is their blanket.

The creek of coldness
shakes your hand
as it turns
blue.
Quickly I pull out
with cold
ripples
where I was.

The winter chills
the quiet creek.
That blizzard
rushed away
the noise.
I need the
Spring
to come.

~ *Lyle Loder Friedman, age 8*

THE GENTLE RIVER

Joy Han, age 12

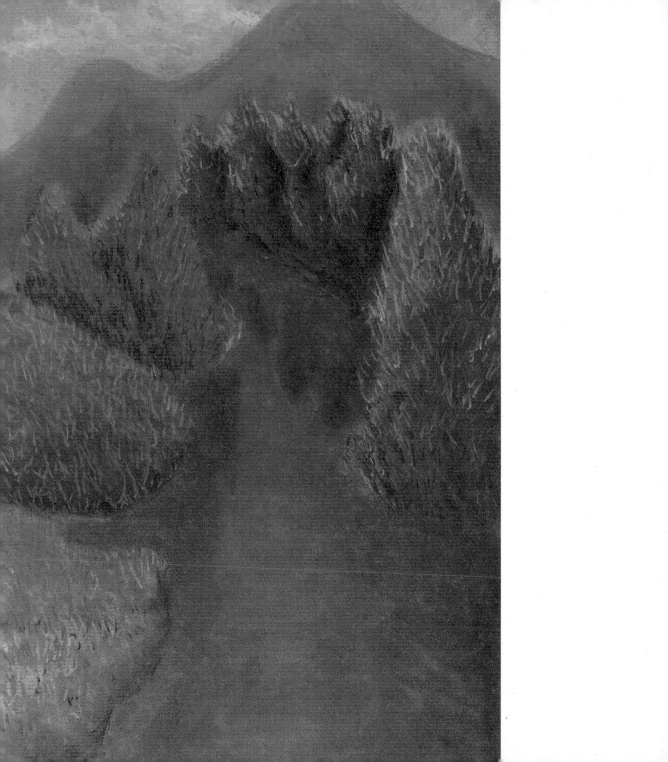

THE EVENING CREEK

Sit in the brush
with your straw hat on
and watch the creek.

Then get up and walk
on the banks, moonlit
with scattered touch-me-nots.

Walk closer to the creek,
and let the mud feel soft
on your bare feet.

Stop to look at jewelweed.
Hear the owl call.
Then dip your hand
into the pure water of the creek.

Walk home
with the taste of the sweet creek
in your mouth.

~ *Suzi Alvarez, age 8*

WATERFALL SLAM

Waterfalls are beautiful
and very fun to watch.

I give them different names
and here's what they are:
        Slam-dinga, Fringa-do, Yabadabado.

Sun rises nice and easy, blooming,
        touching, clear white, coloristic,
        banging, and most important
                beautiful.

The name doesn't matter
        I am just glad it is *waterfall, waterfall*
                waterfall.

~ *Luiz Mendez, age 9*

JUST IMAGINE

Just imagine
Waking up one day,
Looking out your window starting to say...

NO BAD SMELLS
NO SMOKE
NO NOISE
NO TRASH
NO CROWDED PLAYGROUNDS, BASKETBALL COURTS,
OR CORNERS LOADED WITH TEENS
NO BAD WORDS ON THE WALLS AND SIDEWALKS
NO JUNK
NO MUDDY WATERS

NO HUNGER
NO POOR
NO PEER PRESSURE
NO ENVY
NO NAME CALLING

NO GUNS
NO FEAR
NO PAIN
NO MURDER
NO DRUGS

NO DEAD BIRDS BECAUSE OF
NO DEAD GRASS BECAUSE OF
NO DEAD TREES BECAUSE OF
NO DEAD PEOPLE BECAUSE OF
NO PLACE TO PLAY BECAUSE OF

CLEAN UP!
CARE!
HELP EACH OTHER!
PLAY!
GO OUTSIDE AND PLAY!
RUN!
SKIP!
JUMP!
RIDE!
SMILE!
BE HAPPY!
BE SAFE!

And just imagine being a kid
Living by the Anacostia River.

~

El'jay Johnson, age 8

WIT AND FRIGHT

(A poem for two voices)

words for owl	*words for mouse*
Sleep all through the day, at night capture your prey.	
	Savor the sun, it's almost noon, darkness is coming soon.
In your eyes, lanterns burn bright, their golden rays illuminate the night.	
	Scrunched down low, trying to hear,
	your eyes ablaze with fear.

Flying, flying up
in dark pools of sky.

Dark shadow hides the
light
not a speck of moon in
sight

Dinner

Gone

~

Eric Pierson, age 10

HERON

High
on two silver legs
blue ice cream
tipped wings
stretching
golden vanilla
beak
creamy white neck
bent over shimmering water
silky smooth
peach fuzz wings
flooded
with a perfect
golden
ray of light
even stars
back way at its beauty.

~ *Abigail Hemenway, age 10*

THE ANACOSTIA RIVER: WE MAKE A DIFFERENCE

Toiling under the hot sun
Our work has just begun.
Hands moving rhythmically
As sweat pours from our bodies.
Piece by piece we make a difference.

We move in rows along polluted shores
Where flowers no longer grow.
Picking up yesterday's trash
Paper, containers, bottles, cans.
Step by step we make a difference.

We arrive at sunrise
Black bags in hand
Determination in our minds.
We leave behind at sunset only footprints and a beautiful place.
Day by day we make a difference.

Someday the Anacostia River will no longer be suffocated by trash.
Its crystal waters will teem with fish.
Its banks will be crowded with luscious plants.
And its beauty will stun the world
Because we have made a difference.

~ *Sabrina Snell, age 11*

NEW BEGINNINGS

Jazz is like me
skipping rocks through
the sea,
floating to the moon,
dreaming of being alone
in the dark
with only starlight
to guide me.

I am wishing for someone
new to show me the way of hope, the way
of happiness.
I am sitting watching
the sunlight like a bird

watches her eggs, like a museum
watches its diamonds,
like the ocean skipping rocks

back to me, but only I can see the joy
of the sea's waves moving through the music,
the violin moving to a new beat.

~ *Shyann Graham, age 11*

MY PRAYER WISH
Jerrika Shi, age 9

NORTH CAROLINA

In the countryside of North Carolina it's beautiful.
The sun is like a giant star during the day lighting
the world up, telling everybody, "Hi, I'm back."

In the countryside of North Carolina the trees
are bright, green, swishing, dancing back and forth
in the wind's strong breeze. "The cold is coming."

In the countryside of Charlotte, North Carolina
right across the street from Aunte A'Minda's house
is a pond with snakes and fishes in it. "Catch me if you can."

In the pond there are weeds that sway side to side
as quiet as smoke, as gentle as fur.

~ *Jalesha Robertson, age 11*

POTOMAC

Potomac
when we men needed you
you came
like a restive giant from the farther hills
and rent the sunburned earth to make your bed
Potomac
when we men muddied you with boots
and tramped across your waiting waters
you were patient
for our boys
fighting for what they thought was just
brother against brother
on the same brown soil
Potomac
when we men built upon you
with bridges of massive steel
you retreated, silent
to rest beneath the bridge
the sleeping giant
Potomac

when we men muddied you
you watched and did not act
for it was our turn now
to move the earth and shake the iron
      and steel
to free the sleeping giant from our
      clutches
before we rise and find you gone
over the darkened hills of yesteryear
Potomac
the sleeping giant beneath the bridge

~ *Alexandra Petri, age 12*

183

I AM SONG

I am a sparrow black as night
I am a trout swimming in the sea
I am the fireworks in the sky
I am a soccer ball being kicked
I am a polka dance
I am Italy
I am a red tulip
I am spinach   fear me
I am a weeping willow
I am a monsoon
I am New Year's

~

Alex Marrero, age 13

PRAYER

Often have I come to you
In the fitful light of evening
Or the constant sheen of morning
And often have I sought your solace,
River.
Show me the secret of your solitude
That thing, that unknown certain thing
Which has brought you through a hundred shifting seasons
And will bring you through at least a thousand more.
Teach me to be alone through summer, autumn, winter, spring
And still to catch the gleaming sunset
And dance in golden eddies in the shadow of the islands.
Tell me all the secrets of those silent seasons
Or one thing only—
When spring comes, show me how to break the ice.

~ *Alexandra Petri, Age 14*

A RAIN OF YOU

In the deeps of your eyes
Quiet rains sing.
A thousand tuneful whispers:
Each tear a note beyond any cadence of mine.
We have walked
Together as one and a half,
When a salty downpour made a poem
     from the grays of the parking lot.
With each splash of a car through a puddle,
Our extra half became quite mathematically larger.
And even more clouds were forming.
You explained to me
That each drop is its own universe,
Perfectly shaped,
· More beautiful (and important) than yours or mine.
Each drop is a complete prayer
As it plummets toward the asphalt.
We have walked
In the misty rains of a parking lot
As my clunky-heeled shoes
Shattered the surface tension of worlds.
The leather has since dried.
In the deeps of your eyes,
Quiet, thoughtful rain forms
Sweet salinity
Like other tastes I have forgotten.

~ *Anat Ben-Zvi, age 16*

GEESE OVER MENDON PONDS

They came upon us
like I, as a small child,
was always afraid
that a tornado would,
a black mass in the sky,
roaring and cackling,
the occasional high-pitched squeal
like metal on bone.
There were thousands of them,
far more than was necessary,
as if, in the sparse winter,
nature was indulging a little.

~ *Anna Dumont, age 16*

SWIMMING SUMMER

Winding
down a slow maple-syrup snake
she shucks her skin to either side,
slicks the moss and sweetens the trees.
Summer crystallizes in the drops that
spatter her banks.
The old black inner tube is hot,
sucks at your skin, ripples over hers
slow and steady as the shadows of clouds,
as a tongue over smooth lips.

In places,
grayish scum drifts
among the tree roots that peer over the clay and sand.
You can see flies' wings if you look closely in the froth
because they refract the dim leaf light
but you prefer to watch the water
when it breaks open to sky and sun and
the arching concrete bridges.
They lift high and bare, like ribs, deserts,
gasps.

They say the river burns red-golden
from the sap of the cedar trees in mountains
that you've never seen;
you prefer to think of
hot honey,
molten amber,
swimming summer.

~ *Diana Chien, age 16*

FIRE IN WINTER

The hoofprints of the deer
in the snow are broken hearts,
bowed raindrops,
birds' eyes painted with a bamboo brush.

The rough-furred, coal-tipped legs mince:
matchstick pistons, they
strike sparks from iced boulders,
strike a wintry rhythm to the tick and whisper of
the creeping hoarfrost,
the pliant ice sheathing
river stones' flanks.

The scent of resin and musk is in those wide nostrils,
the leaf-shaped ears flick
to catch a memory of soft rain in summer greenery.

Now—a pine bough splits in the distance,
graced with snow's heavy embrace:

There is the sound of my heart.
There is the sound of explosion
as the deer bounds up and out,
heels kicking a spray of diamond-colored fire.

~ *Diana Chien, age 17*

SPRINGWATER HILL

In the stillness of summer
warm waves of sunlight rippled against my face—
I was the first that day to feel them.
The field waved with the breeze,
the tips of the tall grass swept my arms.
Smelling pine, I tasted sap in my mouth.
Walking through the field, I felt the milkweed pods
brush up against my legs;
miniature Pandora's boxes, waiting to ripen.
Light shone off the creek and danced
amongst the leaves above me.
I laughed to myself. The busyness of spring was gone,
and the slow of fall was in the distance.

~ *Rebecca Miller, age 17*

FESTIVAL DAY

it started as a good day
the water was moving smooth
it wasn't all crazy with the gleam
of the sun walking along the bridge to Cape Verdian
festival that happens once every two years music
all day to the red water at sunset here it's dark
there it is clear but my grandmother doesn't talk
about it they came after dark twenty of them twenty of us
with more coming because everyone likes a fight
the flood of the fight rushing from near the water
to the street the sunlight just about gone you
can't change this

~ *Leeron Silva, age 17*

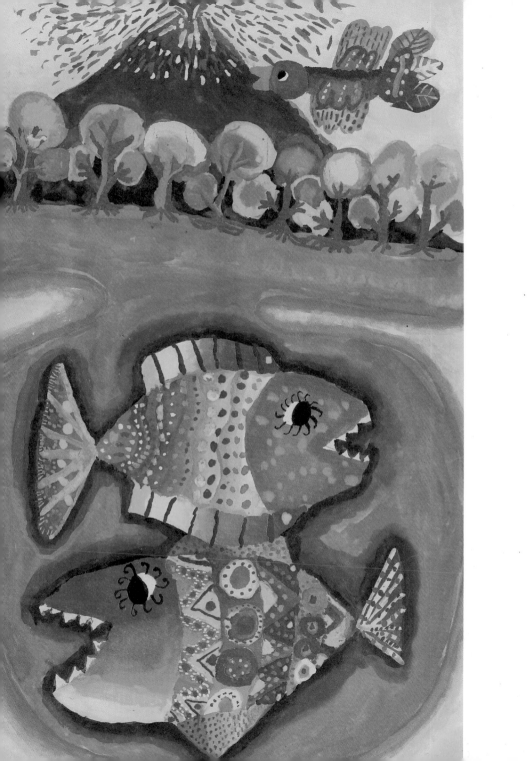

RIVERS

Rivers splatter,
hitting rocks below.
But don't be afraid,
there is poetry
deep inside each crevice.

~ *José Pérez, age 7*

FISHING ON THE OUACHITA

I burn my lure beneath the surface,
Cordell Red Fin, real as a rainbow
you like to feast on.

Starving striped bass
cruising for a bleeding shad,
you rise swift as white gulls above me,
deep from your blue hidden kingdom.

I wait for the moment
when I feel your strike
like a flood swallowing a levee.

Your fight breaks the water,
silver courage stronger than this line.
It gives, you take,
becoming my wish for another day.

~ *Tyler Sellers, age 8*

THE SIMPLE LIFE

The crossroads to heaven make you feel like stones.
The roots of your ashes are like mountains.
The dirty country road makes the sky ahead look yellow.
The kingdom of green blooms in a special red way.
The fog upon the pond is in silence unknown
only two people know the stairs to roses.
My father floats in the air traveling like steel
making echoes that are getting closer.
The crickets make way to stars,
the stars are like traffic on an old silvery, rainy day, and
it is hard to breathe on the fountain of life or death.

~

Scott Laffler, age 9

HEAVEN'S TRUTH

The turtle's shell awaits the fog of the morning.
The beavers sleep quietly in their dirty den.
The stones are surrounded by filthy grass on the riverbank.
The snake's prey is slowly dragged into the winter's snow.
The frosty sleet drizzles in the rapids.
The mist of the river is like a duck's autumn.
In the glow of the morning a squirrel jumps
from pebble to pebble
just like jumping from
sunrise to sundown.
In the wave's darkness, I rest next to the windy stream.
The moonlight glows on the oyster's cave.
The soil covers the moist leaf.
The pine trees sing a never-ending song
to the end of the poem's shadows.

~ *Scott Laffler, age 10*

SWEETWATER[*]

Beads of silver plummet from the sky
And are caught for a moment in the fingers of swaying pines.
Then, the drops fall to my brow,
Cooling the afternoon heat
Before disappearing into the crushed quartz,
Quartz brought by an ancient glacier.
Seeking to hold the riches in my hand
I hike on as if a treasure map were given.
I walk among the giant magnolias, turkey-foot oaks,
Beneath a canopy of pines, near a carpet of wildflowers.
I brush against the red cedars and smell distant memories.
Hiking down the hill
I enter the wet bottomland,
Where animals make their homes.
After crossing the bog on hurricane-fallen trees
I climb a gentle rise then down,
Following the magical sound I hear.
It is the rushing of water.
It is Sweetwater Creek.
Kneeling on the sandy shore of white
I see again the liquid silver.
Like an explorer of old,
I reach down and hold the treasure in my cupped hands.

~ *Christa Glover, age 10*

* *Sweetwater Creek empties into Juniper Creek. The Juniper enters into the Blackwater River. Sweetwater Creek is in the Blackwater State Forest in northwest Florida. It is a clear, wild, and unpolluted stream.*

SWAMP SHACK

The shack
Sitting on squat pillars
Tall cypress looming over
Separated
From the swamp
Filled inside
With potions and powders of a *traiteuse*
Cajun remedies
At all time
She is ready for anything
Even the raccoons and squirrels
On the bank
Wait
For a dose of magic.

~

Allison Alford, age 12

LOUISIANA MORNING

Let morning come.
Let the gators wake.
Let the birds sing to the sun.
Let morning come.

Let the morning come.
Let the brown pelican
Swoop down to eat its breakfast,
Let the cypress knees bend to stretch again.
Let morning come.

Let morning come.
Let the baby's cries
Wake the mother
To wake the father.
Let morning come.

Let morning come.
Let the pirogues begin to swim in the bayou.
Let the morning come.
Let morning come.

~ Sarah Spain, age 11

UNTITLED
Gavid Muradov, age 9

MY LOUISIANA

The breeze
Lifts my hair
And
I do a dance
With the wind
The tall grasses
Waltz
With the cattails
And the cricket's song
Skips
In the air
Like a bow on a fiddle
This is my Louisiana

~ *Emily Bush, age 12*

HURRICANE

It's like living in a movie
The massive beast is here
We stare off the porch
The wind tugs the great oak
By its golden hair
Trees dance in the wind
Skies gray
Like moldy bread
Our palm trees
Lash their arms
Grabbing the earth
Leaves and twigs like
Mosquitoes
Everywhere

Destruction—
The road paved with
Oak, birch, and pine—
Signs strewn
Here and there
Another of life's storms

~ *Chelsea Bagwell, age 13*

ROCKEFELLER WILDLIFE PRESERVE: MID-AUGUST

The air is moist
The water bittersweet
A southern gulf breeze sighs
Laughing gulls call
And cicadas click their
Luminous song
I smell the death scent
Of beached gars
And see the dreamy haze
Of oil on water
Nearby an alligator stares
With tabby eyes
A great heron startles
From its marsh bed
Standing on the rip-rap,
I peer at the water
And slowly hoist
The turkey neck on string

A bluepoint crab
Grips the bait
I slyly dip the net
A good two feet away
And scoop up the crustacean
Without warning
And drop it into a bucket
To meet many friends,
Gifts of the Mississippi,
The day has reached its climax
Animals sleep through the heat,
Hiding in the wax myrtles
A snowy egret,
White plumage glistening,
Glides into the roseau cane.

~ *Kevin Maher, age 12*

TO MY FATHER

The spouseless
Tangerine
Slowly descends
Toward rippling gray waters
The sea cradles him
Like a newborn child

The stars begin to peek
By twos and threes
From the massive
Somber blanket
Aloft

The full moon
Illuminates me
I can see myself
And faraway
Into the coming hours

The waters cleanse
My filthy hands
Of wounds and scars
Heal me
Feel me

Lend me your voice
Oh surging river
Sing of my love

~ *Kara Guarisco, age 13*

206

GARDENS

In this vast, pleasant zoo
I see perfection
Of Grecian delight,
Tiers of straight walkways and paths
Line the solid labyrinth.
A forest, so trimmed in its
Cordiality
Bows like a handsome butler
In the rustling air.
Statues amusing,
Hidden among the bushes,
Toadstools of cement
Plastered into the water.
I see people trying to create
The perfect nature,
And I see nature
Declaring a silent war.

~ *Wujun Ke, age 14*

BEHIND THE LIGHT HOUSE HOTEL

Gulf Shores, home, tradition.
Brightly painted VW Beetles and Jeeps
Cruise the strip—gift stores, surf shops,
And that club, The Pink Pony Pub.
Hotel parking lot, broken shells for turf,
Spring breakers just back from Panama City
Still decked in shorts, T-shirts, & sandals.
The tepid salt air fans across the sound,
Kicking up the corners of blankets, beach towels
Scattered along the white beach.
Clear water as far as Cuba and the Yucatán Peninsula.
Dolphins jest and jump in the distance, not too far
Shrimp boats and oil tankers.

Cute boys with built bodies skimboard along the shore
Surf rolls in, kissing toes, sucking silt back with it,
Palm trees and starfish fingered gingerly onto the sand
By a teenage girl uncomfortable in her two-piece,
Eye candy for a schoolboy
Just out for a short holiday.
Sun sets slowly in the west,
The beach abandoned by seven,
Overtaken by jellyfish,
Sand crabs, and miniature hermits.
Like ebb and flow,
Tomorrow will be the same.

~ *Amanda Miller-Hudson, age 14*

PECAN ISLAND

The sun's glamorous rays
break through the early morning fog
like arrows through air.
I sit in a blind,
wiggling my toes to keep warm
from winter's defiant chill.
The Lab returns from the pond
with the fresh scent of mud on her back.
The sun fades my invisibility
and animals are aware of my presence.
My deepest regards to the numerous teal
that have fallen to the bangs and blasts
of my shotgun—
but the taste of fresh duck is unforgiving.

~ *Parker Reaux, age 14*

NATURE SLEEPS

The mountains, the rocks, the peaks
Are sleeping,
Uplands hush
Thousands of swamp things are still,
Creatures under every bush
Crouch, and the bees
Rest in their honeyed ease,
In the sea fish swim,
And each bird folds its wings over its head.

~ *Rafael Espinoza, age 14*

MY RIVER

Stanislav Shpanin, age 10

US MEN

waterproofed to the waist
see a vision, that to us
only comes once a year.
We are grumbling, stalking
out to the shed, to the purr
of engines warming.
Our breath spirits the chilled wind.
All day, work.
For the first time I am a part of it,
deserving of the reward that will come.
We sink back into cold metal bunkers
dug along gumbo levees
the color of potter's clay.
Dried stalks & weeds sway as cover.
In the distance, floodwater
rises against the sunburst ray
of a dying day. I hear the geese faintly
honk & gaggle above me. I see silhouettes
dot the horizon. There are splashes
of touch & go, wings flapping.
Yes, I do hope they like it here.
My father reaches for his boy,
and I give in.

~ *Eric Wiesemann, age 15*

BLIND MORNING

My morning seizure
stifles the siren
from second bunk I descend

As always I've
left warmth for the promise
of consciousness

I do not
share the enthusiasm
of my coffee

We trace the trail
to first light trample soy
and scatter rice

Noises of
eighteen-wheelers on the
      highway
the earth's breath

Slight are the sun's rays
only the shivering rice pond
stays the stars' strength

From evolution's
grip we take
natural selection

In the wake
of the expanding universe
two teal on the left

~ *Kevin Maher, age 15*

213

ODE TO A RIVER EVENING

After the rain, the river is still easy.
Hundreds of mosquitoes
Cover the banks like draped blankets.

Trees try to overlook the moon.
It darkens. The mosquitoes thin out.
They have had their share of water.

Moonlight seeps through leaves.
Ripples shimmer. Near the water
Mosquitoes tease a fish.

They follow its silver waves.
Full and content, the fish fades.
The water now murky,

No more light or movement,
Just the sound of water, still.

~ *Jamie Trog, age 15*

AFTERMATH

Oak leaves float on water
From the trees that once stood tall, firmly rooted in history
Stagnant water that was formerly a powerful river
Now submerses the pavement
And houses
And people
Of this once-great city
Grandmother's lace
Tinted with age, smelling of lavender flowers
Taken out of its resting place
In the bureau drawer
Now it lies in the dirty street
Soon to be erased from memory
Along with the other remnants
Of this broken metropolis

~ *Susan Storey, age 15*

FLOWING INTO THE RIVER ONE DAY

I am here to watch the river
sitting here on hay bale, legs crossed, head
covered sun warm, wind chilly
hands gloved
mind open
Geese high above
fly, having left their place of slumber
when awakened with untimely
chorus of people sounds
Mother sits with her mother,
at the base of my feet, talking the
two of them, about dogs, and pig manure,
and cockleburs
Friend (best) beside me, hushing
my sister (who will not stop
the wheels in her mouth from running it seems)
Hill we sit on crest of is stubble
corn covered, unshaven face of late
February

Reeds by river lean inward, drinking endless bounty
watchful, yes, accepting, no, but humbled by winter
Mud green and brown lines the bank of the river old
friend
older still than me, or dogs, or sister, or
bright cool day
River cuts my view in half, blue, gray, silver
twisting its way along until it no longer belongs to
me
flowing into the minutes
with grace

~ *Elizabeth Clark, age 15*

GUTTER DUTY

I am not gifted with the foresight
To determine in some great act of jurisprudence
Whether that section of earth is yours, mine, ours.
It's a shame Epimetheus was unable to see
The two of us, in bright yellow raincoats,
Run gray in torrential rain,
Raising our voices above thunder
Over who would clear the gutter.

In the waters that ran black with murky darkness
I thought I saw a flash of silver
A charm from my childhood.
But you, you saw the concrete box
That framed the urban river
And commented on how it reeks
With a delicate sort of hauteur.

In the type of gust that forces a hand on your head
To keep your hat from lifting off
We're muttering our hate of Spring
And feverishly scratching at clumps
Of natural pollution, those baby-green leaves,
To liberate the rain rivers.

The two of us are urban tadpoles, I think
We're swimming in a pool of Oceanids, as if
Oceanus and Tethys really did
Fill the world with their love.
It makes me a cynic to push the blasted leaves aside
And watch the water flee.
It makes me wish I was hydraulic.

~ *Jenny Fan, age 16*

DOWN DEEP

It's cold and quiet down deep
50, 60, 70 feet
Just the steady, hollow sound of
    your breath
Lets you know you're living
Push, pull, push, pull
Everything is alive
From the timid, bug-eyed squirrelfish
    to the stinging coral
You are obsolete
You are merely a ship's shadow or
    a passing cloud
Something that blots out the sun
    then passes on
You are clunky, metal, awkward
They are sleek, slender, efficient
It is not as colorful as you expected
No bright reds or pinks
The sun cannot penetrate deep
    enough for that
As it rightly shouldn't
The sun is far smarter than you
If she wanted, the sun could point out
    every rainbow-backed sea slug
Or Technicolor trumpet fish

But then you wouldn't leave
Never go back to your world
    of grays and browns
    and blacks
You would claim the ocean
As you did every other beautiful
    place
Fish moved to reservations
Forced to give up their coral
    palace for a flat,
    sandy wasteland
No, the sun knows better
She will keep the beaches warm
She will make the shallow water
    glisten
But she will leave it cold and quiet
    down deep

~ *Lindy Muse, age 16*

{ **CYCLE OF LIFE** }
Yann Lee, age 17

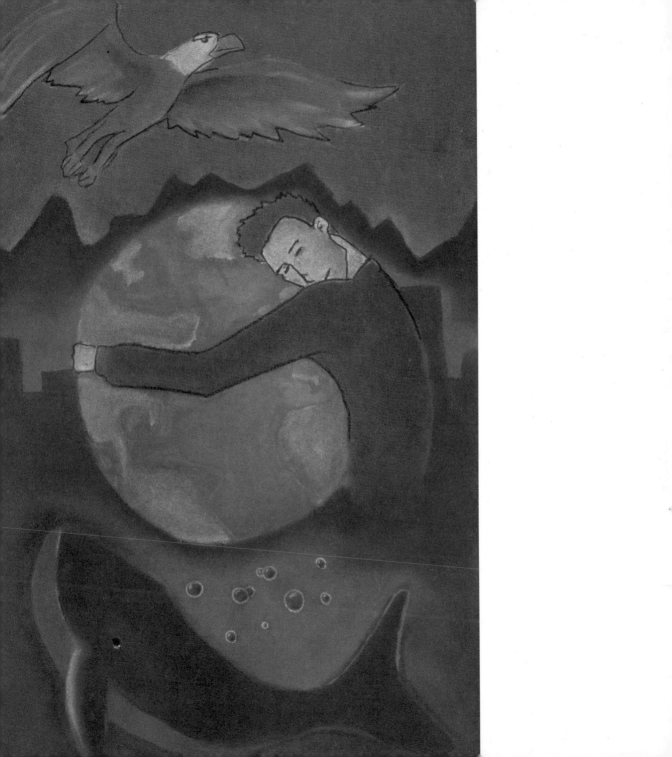

RIVER HISTORIES

In the river's deep heart
a forked stick strains from the water
like the fingers of a Nile woman who,
last century,
touched them to her forehead,
then plunged them into rushing swiftness;
beads of sweat flying past her still,
stick folding under,
acquiescing.

On the river's still bank
footprints lead up the soil where
a family of ducks plodded last season,
perfect webbed fossils getting smaller,
smaller as water droplets splash them,
muddy them, make them fall back,
get up again
and again.

On the river's sturdy log
forming a bridge over water, a friend
sits and shows me where her father led
horses. Where she puts her feet in,
the currents curl her toes forward.
I look to her face—a smile of histories,
her eyes the color
of the river.

~ *Rebecca Givens, age 15*

LETTER TO THE ARCHITECT

Not even you can keep me from
mentioning the fish, their beauty of
scaled brevity, their clipped-swishing
tails funneling in everything animal.
Wintertime when I saw them, their
pursed old ladies' mouths, gaping under
pooled clarity to share some gulled-up gossip.
Their bones, pure equilateral, poked stripes
at base and height, bereft of architects' errors
or human compensation. I remembered then
your last letter; you wrote you couldn't cut
another mitre, solder another joint, peel
another bit of glue from between your fingertips.
I'm going to crack soon, you said.
There must be some way to perfection
in this grasping for centimeters. The stick
will stay straight, the model be done,
done beautifully and done well someday.
I wrote back—I only know the cod with their
paling rib bones, their geometry unwarped by cold.
I know their tunnels dug frost-time underwater,
their crossings of snowflake symmetry. When
the thaws come, their finned bodies filter
the halfway ice like clean spectra.
You must know—the sight is exquisite.
If only I could give the gift of fish-making
in as many words as this.

~ *Rebecca Givens, age 16*

RIVERS ON TITAN

These lines in the photo
Do not do the rivers justice

Trails long dried
Still captivate—this
Century-old muse of scientists.

In my mother's newly wrinkled smile
I glimpse my own skin.

I am the placid canyons of Saturn's moon,
In her chasms' muted cries,
I hear the Monday rain.

~ *Ting Gou, age 16*

BENEATH THE OAK

Crouched beneath the live oak,
embracing arms shelter me.
Entangled fingers reach out,
each wanting to be the first to ruffle
my crown of thick raven hair.
Leaf shadows dance
the tango around my brown Nikes;
the movement growing faster,
then slowing with the
breath of a breeze.
Noon steadily approaches.
A gummi wrapper among the leaves:
graffiti desecrating a sacred world.
My name fills my ear;
I turn and rise in answer.
A backward glance reveals leaves
waltzing to fill the place where my body had been.
Yet another layer beneath the oak.

~ *Stephen Brunet, age 16*

DEAR NIGHT,

I must tell you, silence
      is no longer the virtue it once was, rather
it only reminds us how small and alone we
      really
are. Next time you wish us to celebrate a
      cosmic event, please,
be more direct. A comet, or a meteor shower,
      even some good old-fashioned fireworks. The star
was a nice touch, I must admit:
      more suited to the taste of poor mortals than this
awful,
      divine
         stillness.

~ *Sarah Dooley, age 16*

BERWICK

I am from the brown water in a lake caged
From the Corps' walls that greet the sun
I am from the cabin on the water
And the hand-built dock, littered with extensions of friends
I am from the tall cypress that move with the wind
From the hushed conversations the willows have with morning
I am from the fog off the water
And the winds from the south
I am from wax myrtles, hydrangeas and the scent of burnt sulfur
I am from the mismatched eyes of our faithful Catahoula
And the crisp boat rides, trying to outrun December's chill
I am from the Basin, watching the sun fall below the wall of man

~ *Billy Creed, age 16*

WATER

Water glistens on the rocks,
Flowing down to the sea,
Gurgling, splishing, splashing, crashing,
Never stopping
For a cup of tea.

~

Helena Leech, age 7

HIGHLAND SPRING

Winking water squeals
Rinsing pebbles' dirty faces,
Reflecting horizon.

~

Ruth Warren, age 11

GREAT GRIZZLY BEAR
Jackson Darham, age 10

CHLORINATION

Green tangles of
seaweed courting our
bony ankles in waist-high depths
ended our
lakeside excursions.

You accused the water
of being dirty when you saw the seagulls
and cursed the piercing stones of the water's
eroded floor in
girlish tongues.

I liked people watching
and buying artificial
sugar-laden frozen treats and letting
the big kid pump the well,
washing the soft clinging
mud from my red-hot feet.

But then we began
a daily ritual of
skipping across
a scorching suburban street
toward the neighbor's fenced yard,
replacing sand
with concrete, and letting you
spend days afloat
pure toilet-blue water while I
sat immersed on the steps,
unable to touch the tiled bottom.

~ *Meghan Sitar, age 17*

THE LAKE

I have given the world a ceiling—
Dark, cold, rippling—
Lying there in the water
With my head tilted back

My body thanks
The top of my head
For were it not in the ceiling
I would fall into nothing
Into everything

We've been told that beyond the sky is space
An unending ocean
Of things unknown
And known

If I would drop
Like ripe fruit from a tree
(When I can no longer hold on)
Would I fall forever?

~ *Taylor Volkman, age 17*

BAYOU II

Below me, a rickety wooden rowboat,
damp in the fog,
rests embedded in a world
beneath the muddy swampland waters.
Egrets paint the landscape,

gliding with ease to the nearest branches.
Crawfish wriggle
to escape a tattered prison of trellised thread.
The moist air swirls with silence
magnifying the softest sounds of life,
faintly whispering the songs of
home home home.

~ *Jaime Glas, age 17*

LAST YEAR IN MONTCLAIR

last year
I left a ballpoint pen
in a park in Montclair
and last week it wrote to me a letter
saying it missed our
Sunday crosswords
and the way I signed my name

"my last name is Coleman now"
it said
and told me of the man
who used my pen for signing checks
and contracts
and kept it in a pressed blue suit
beside his hundred-dollar bills

I wrote back
with an awkward pause
as I introduced my new pen
(who was thinner
and stayed inked longer)
and I admitted with regret
that the local paper
no longer ran our crossword

I promised that we would get together
sometime
for coffee, write a letter to the paper
for old times' sake

~ *Isaac Graf, age 17*

234

ON THE BASIN

The old tire swing
Suspends me over the water at my folks' camp,
My feet wallowing in the Atchafalaya.
I wonder how it's possible for this ancient oak
To weather the urge to finally surrender and fail me,
To plunge me into the constant swashing of water
Eroding its purchase,
Loosening its rooty grip on the soggy bank.

One day long ago, Grandmom and Pop
Tattooed him with a new pocketknife.
Today, the sunlight paints a silky finish on the sky
Toward which I swing,
Flying away with the summer birds.

~ *Meagan Michalk, age 17*

BEYOND MY WINDOW

The trees are naked now
Remnants of their summer blankets litter the ground
Unembarrassed by their bare bodies they stand tall
Limbs reach with bony fingers for cryptic reasons
The crisp bite of the evening air makes me shiver
But not them
How odd the trees are
Their boldness to stand and be noticed
To go exposed in the coldest part of the year
They need no coat or woolen socks
This is their time to be seen
I can see them dance beyond my window at night
An elaborate and arcane ballet
Swaying in cadence with the wind
They throw parties every now and then
All birds welcome
Rest on our shoulders
You have quite a journey yet
In the summer they rest
Slumber beneath a quilt of green

~ *Daniel Koepp, age 17*

THIS IS HOW NATURE WORKS

First she boils
her primordial broth
eager to please
her fickle husband
Fate
who sips

"Too plain."

So she grows
garden-variety veggies
seeking to satisfy
her fickle husband
Fate
who spoons

"Not hearty enough."

Then she cuts
the choicest meats
focused on filling
her fickle husband
Fate
who spears

"Needs flavor."

Now she reaps the rankest of
weeds
aiming to avenge
the abuses of
her fickle husband
Fate
who spits

"Too saucy."

And empties the pot.

~ *Johanna Chotiwat, age 17*

I AM FROM

I am from a world of mischief
from accidental backyard fires
and hidden tree fortresses which lay above the world of reality
where the sap made my fingers sticky and the
woods soaked my shirt with the smell of pine.

I am from excavated hidden treasures,
the honeysuckles beyond the backyard and the berries deep in
the bushes which always trickled my mouth with a bittersweet
surprise. I revealed the cattails' plush interior and the free spirit
of daffodils being tossed about my head by the power of a
gentle spring breeze.

I am from accident-prone adventures:
I have felt the piercing stab of a pond's intensely frigid waters as
sheets of ice break below;
I have been pounded by the weight of a vending machine as my
curiosity suffocated my senses.

I am from a unique family,
the values and cultures of many worlds integrated within one
household.
Expressive Norwegian art flared with the rustic artifacts of
Peruvian ruins,
the collaboration which keeps a home consistent and secure
through the wear and tear of multiple moves.

I am from the memories.
I am from the hikes to spiritual waterfalls and eye-opening
vacations to the places and lives of my ancestors.
I make all these memories; therefore, I come from me.

~

Caroline Greene, age 17

UNWELCOMING WILD

I.

It was in the paper,
The story about the missing boy
Who became lunch for a ten-foot gator,
And the one about the family
Who found the girl's body floating
Near the bank, shredded like silk.
No one praises these
Primitive mothers and fathers,
Nor compliments their eyeing care,
Protecting their young
With stroking confidence as they slide
Belly first into the river,
A deep, mud-swollen vision
Of the wild—unwelcoming wild.

II.

The loon's home is not his own,
Not the way it was
When the fish-catching bird went south.
Summer is near,
The thawed-through ice now a river.
The diamond-shaped eddies reflect
What life is for—survival.
The living log rises,
Shares a staring moment
Eye to eye. The exhausted loon
Decides it's time to find another home.

~ *Jaime Brame, age 17*

I GOT THE BLUES
Gerald Allen, age 13

DEAR AQUARIUS,

Tonight you bend
because the stars are fearless
enough to glow on you
They speak their truths in muted light
If one grain of sand is traced from a
twisting kiss in the North
to this forgiveness draped around my feet
then salvation lies in every loop and thrash
You keep your secrets well
in lengthy, passionate channels,
too gargling and gracefully
knitted to control
But Aquarius, I have
long held this view of you
basking in your semiprecious charm
When I was small, seven or so,
I'd put on brother's dingy jeans
and rill my way through silted grass
to the steady saplings
blooming at your edge
Toe by toe, foot by dirtied foot
I disappeared
Everything from the mirror down
was me no more

~ *Kt Harmon, age 17*

BROKEN

I stand on a pile of broken cypress
Winter's hand still grabbing my breath

The exhale lingers, frozen above my head
A memorial, reminding me of what it's like to be out here

In the distance is an oxbow
Surrounded by thousands of nature's sentinels

The sound of wings on top of a coming darkness
Breaks my comfort-induced abstraction

To the right, the wind's trickery
Chases the water out of the lake

To the left, an eagle breaks its circle
Folding itself into the brown waves

The water shudders with a massive weight lifted
The pelicans make it off the water and deep into the stars of
Zydeco country

~ *Billy Creed, age 17*

SUBMERGED

this is a reflection of a beginning
the result of a momentary insanity,
a one-minute bravery.
I stood next to you out of curiosity.
three a.m. standing in black,
under one thousand stars
rushing from the left into the clouds.
clothes drenched in remnants of the Cahaba River,
heavy legs dragging in the sand.
you stumbled,
I followed.

heaven forbid, you fall into the water
like that;
cold, vulnerable,
free,
but I never learned to swim,
and I knew you wouldn't jump.
words limped pathetic
between one lip and the other.
languages mocked impotent
and useless.

still you spoke,
thoughtful, yet careless.
i stood next to you out of curiosity,
out of late night,

I stood next to you out of curiosity,
out of carpe diem
mentality.
and this place is already
out of this world.
held softly between banks

I stood next to you out of curiosity.
you fell into
the water, so i
jumped in.

~ *Sarah E. Ponder, age 17*

SHRIMPING

Laughter on the water, at the dock, cast and pull,
music of water and voices.
Salt water in the mouth, taste the river mud.
Reach for the net, arm goes down, hold with your teeth, cast, spin,
and release.
Breathe.
Crash of water. Spray on the wind.

Hand over hand, cast and pull,
laughter at a caught fish, a squid. Stop to watch a heron.
Missed throw, the net twists.
Crash, pull it in, and throw again.
Laughter as a ten-year-old boy tries to throw a fifty-pound net.
Catch him before he goes in.

Sun goes down in the marsh. Light the lamps.
Crickets sing and moonlight reflects off the water.
Moths hum and bump at the lights, shrimp till the tide changes.

Orange fades to blue, night sky. Night on the marsh, the river.
Sit and watch the tide.
Birds cry, marsh smell of salt and water, marsh mud and wood smoke.
Pine bugs whir and scream in the dark. Lap of water on the dock.
Tired voices murmur, soft laughter.
A cool breeze whips wet and tired faces.
Cools the body and the mind.

Pack up the nets; blow out the lamps, head home.
Sit in the kitchen and clean shrimp.
Get kicked out of the kitchen and sit on the porch and clean shrimp.
Pick up by the antenna, pinch off the head.

Old men drinking beer and telling stories.
Flash of cigarettes in the dark, sweet smoke.
Glow of charcoal, hamburgers on the grill.
Old women in the kitchen cracking jokes, laughter as they cook.
Crabs on the stove, coleslaw on the counter, peanuts on the boil.
Life, the river.

~ *Amelia Sides, age 18*

TURTLE BEACH

1,000 megapixels of:

taffy air, grandma sun hats,
pretty princess shovels—
poised and ready to dig

into summer's snow.
A butter-pecan froth,
hang gliding on gravity's goodwill,
238,606 miles below the source;

a mutual relationship:
water and gravity—

g-force beats me into the ground
like the stake of a tent;
I am the parasite.

I could set my watch by it, the tide,
but time left me
—like a sundial after dark—
. . . back in some place called Kokomo.

I change to a telephoto lens.

Now, is it land on water or water on
land?
White on black or black on white?
I can never remember.

I switch to panoramic mode.

The horizon is a myth anyway, anyway.
Just a point where
my eyes end and the sea begins
to stretch her quads.

~ *Bridget Walsh, age 18*

ON FORGETTING

It's easy to forget
                   the air
(so soft and hushed just floating there)

                the moon
(quietly looming moving so slowly
you even don't notice
until it slips off in the morning)

                the sky
(pinned up at night by little pricks of light)

                the trees
(bent piously under the glorious weight
of it all)

                the water
(slithering sinuously and gracefully
light tickling its back)

it's so easy to forget
until one night
you step out and

the moon is a giant circle
punched out of paper by a four-year-old
bold and grinning

the trees reach and sing hallelujah
skies soar up
and the air is so still
that you can almost see
the little breezes that butterfly-kiss your cheek

for a moment the splendor
is crushing.

~ *Catherine Killingsworth, age 18*

RAIN

Lightning dances beneath the tumbling surface
of furrowed, thundering clouds
and suddenly, the fever breaks
droplets pour
and collect in my hands.
Of all the words in the English language
these have fallen together
to form
one small gift.

~ *Bethany Bernard, age 18*

{ RAINING DAY }
Tracey Jen, age 11

SUNDAY AFTERNOON

Pedal hard, hard as you can,
right down the hill, right for the river,
right through the grasses and bushes and grapevines
that hug the edge, line the bank,
and cushion the fifteen-foot fall
to the bottom of the water.
Wheels, wheels, turning and turning past branches and leaves
and honeysuckle, honeysuckle,
smell of honey, sweet,
sharp squares of sun, hot through the trees,
smiling and smiling, turning and turning,
right for the river,
over the edge
of the warmth and the light,
into the water,
chilly and deaf, it runs in the ears,
plunge, sink, like lead in a bathtub

eyes closed ears full hair heavy skin cold air gone hit bottom sail
up break through the surface gasping breathing gasping breathing
and breathing, and breathing,
and dripping
the air is bright and clear, the sun, sweet and warm

~ *Rachel Blumenthal, age 18*

Now is the silence, that cool last
silence before

the mural's skewed, the music cut;

before my ears are abused
        by the rough, vulgar
beep (whirr click) of everything else.
                *
What sweet poetry is
        the spider's web:
life without fanfare and
death without tragedy

played among the deaf silver violin
                strings hung with dew,
so tightly strung beyond
        our understanding.
                *
The little septic pool
flowing back of the house
must babble and rush.

For all the water we don't have

it must be Styx, Nile, Yellow, Amazon—
        with all its extravagant filth.

~ *Tiffanie Jones, age 18*

RIVERBANK SONG

Skipping rocks on the Ohio
Thinking of lots of things
Like the river
Bigger than me

I was eleven
With three friends
I like to call my brothers and sister
Watching the glittering up and down
And two friends
I like to call my parents
Reading from a history brochure

Standing on the very same bank
Where a young entrepreneur named Abe
(At the age I am now, not then)
Began a ferry business
I remember his boat passing by in the setting sun
And there was his silhouette
And there were his wobbly legs
And there I was his friend
With tangly hair in the almost-midwestern wind
And a smooth rock in one hand

And at the age he was then and I am now
I stood in the morning mist with those same friends
And watched Eliza and her baby emerge from the thick river fog
Barefoot on blocks of ice
To freedom on the other side
Which was where I was sitting
One hundred and fifty years later
Breathing breath hot and wet against my scarf

~ *Elizabeth Westby, age 18*

1717 PICAYUNE STREET

Plunged. Into a nightmare
Anxious, tired, hungry we arrived.
It looked like nothing.

Where a proud house once reigned over water oaks
And stood down mausoleums of Confederate dead

A single tree remained.

A towering water oak, with limbs beckoning for nightfall,
Receiving only an august haze, choking fall from its leaves.
Roots that swim through *la terre noire* like ducks on the pond

In the back, it was my tree.
I played on it during those monotonous summers.
Anything to get out of that proud house.
So proud it had no air conditioning,
So proud it had no TV.
Anything to stay away from that graveyard
That ate footballs and came alive with "Dixie" at nightfall.

It used to have a swing.
But now it just has a rope.
Tangled,
Knotted,
Broken.
A lot like our family,
A lot like our city,
A lot like our home.

~ *Billy Creed, age 18*

AT CENTENNIAL OLYMPIC PARK

Let us watch them dance, baby bro
Your little black body nestled
In my side, like a small seal,
The fountain water raining all 'round us
Confetti from a piñata

Thoom-thoom, thoom
Drums beat on naked skins
As they twirl on the watery pavement
Raindrops splashing in slow motion
Over their black, white, yellow, and tan bodies
Syncopation

Thoom-thoom, thoom
Two claps and again they go
Through the five interlocking rings,
Fountains shooting into heaven, fists pumping through skies,
Droplets cascading across waiting tongues

Thoom-thoom, thoom
Do you feel the earth dancing,
Her wide hips grooving?
She gathers in her mighty arms
The wet, crescent footprints shaped like broken souls
Strewn across the pavement

Each stomp breaks away
A chain
Each leap unshackles
A limb

Don't be scared! My arm is around you
In your face, I see my own
These droplets on your bare brown back
Are quivering, not crying
Open your eyes, baby bro,
The world is dancing

~ *Shalini Ramachandran, age 18*

AND YOU DANCE

You are of water,
tiny droplets of light.
The motion in you
a property of liquid.

How do you make your body
glide in such a luminous way
and move in perfect time
to the rhythm of the music,

flowing through us
like water making its way
through even the most
twisted landscapes?

The way you dance is an
elixir, a stunning mixture
of liquid and light,
inviting the hours to slip by.

I want to dance
to the point of liquidity
and have the music brim
from my fingertips, too.

~ *Lauren Carlisle, age 18*

SUMMER SHOWERS

Loren Kim, age 15

263

COLORFUL SHOOTING STAR NIGHT

In Puerto Rico it's midnight.
We are on the beach. My friend Jason is
on his cell phone. I'm tired and looking at the sky.

Out of nowhere I see a blue star
go WHAM like a getaway car. Five minutes
later Jason says, *Junito, look at the shooting star!*

And you didn't believe me before? I say.
We see more colors that night. Yellow,
a brightish white. I wonder if they see

them in the city. The sky that night was
like a flash of snow falling in the streets.

DESTELLOS DE ESTRELLAS FUGACES

En Puerto Rico era medianoche.
Estábamos en la playa. Mi amigo Jason
estaba en el celular. Estaba cansado y
miraba al cielo.

De repente de la nada vio una estrella fugaz
Que hizo Wham . . . como un carro volador.
Cinco minutos más tarde Jason dice,
¡Junito mira la estrella fugaz!

Y no me creíste anteriormente.
Vemos muchos colores esta noche.
El cielo esta noche parece un destello
cayendo sobre las calles.

~ *Carlos Alameda, age 11*

BAIJI*

A flashing white fin appears,
Then vanishes
Into the muddy, light brown waters of the Yangtze River.
Unknown to humankind,
Before Three Gorges Dam began.
The dam in central China on the Yangtze River
Will produce much electricity
But will produce no good for this dolphin.

It swims upstream back to its birthplace on the same river,
To nurture its young,
Much like the salmon.
It cannot see,
But uses vibrations.
The most endangered dolphin in the world.
It will be wiped off the face of the earth
Within a few decades.

The Three Gorges Dam will block off the passage
That these dolphins swim through
To get to the nurturing ground.

The water was once filled with these quick creatures,
Streaks of white whenever you looked hard,
But now, threatened by the dam,
Fewer than fifty are left.
This soon-to-be-extinct dolphin only found in the Yangtze,
This white flash,
Flag bearer,
This dying creature,
Is, indeed,
The *Baiji.*

~ *Christine Yin, age 13*

* *Baiji in Mandarin means "the flag bearer that was left behind."*

WATERSHED LIFE

Floodplain,
Bangladesh,
Totally flat
Except for the Chittagong Hills,
Deforestation but lots of grass;
Hill after hill with the Ganges River swimming by
Like the stream of blood in your body.
Near the split delta,
Sons go fetch water in buckets,
The delta in the south,
The life force for villagers.
And so goes
The Ganges River.
In the many rivers of this fertile land,
One sees little children "skinny dipping,"
Women bathing in their saris.
Others watch them by the lake in the bushes,
Gently laughing with the wind.
Cows moo in the fields,
Farmers work hard in the paddies with sickles,
The housewife cooks dinner for the family
And wears her sari covering the top of her head.

One can barely see her face in the beef curry smoke.
Then, the family gathers and washes their muddy hands,
Each taking the bowl of beef curry and *dahl* after the day's labor
The family chat about the day
And laugh and giggle,
Under the bright, full yellow moon shining on the
Small bamboo hut.
The moonlight reflecting on the Ganges River
Like a happy face in a mirror.

~ *Jeff Hwang, age 13*

LUNCH IN PHUKET, DECEMBER 26TH

Earthspeak:
Rumbled, thundered out the vowels
Sounding of ancient terra
And its dance through the centuries
Shook the resonant sea awake

A seismic wave, sifting the black dirt
Far beneath the ocean in its shimmering basin
Was answered
And the water's flowing dance began—
I rinsed my dishes in the sink

More waves snaked East, then West
The dance quickened in pace
Fishing boats bobbed to aqueous rhythms

Now unsettled, frothing, foaming
Ocean-tossed stars—
White flecks of sea spray
Grasped at the coast
Foamy soap clung at my arms like limpets—
it was my turn to wash up.

And the deep sea strode in
Sprinting now
As its blue green hands
Reached out

And the Tide came in . . .

~ *Madeline Wong, age 13*

I AM A RIVER

I am liquid glass sparkling
pure and innocent,

I am the great ear of the world,
I hear the hurt, anguish, love and hate

I spy on romantic couples,
eavesdrop on father-son conversations

I hear murders being plotted,
see drugs being sold
I witness the slaughter of unarmed creatures

People ask me for advice, wishing,
hoping I have answers

I have heard a million things and am still astonished
by what people have the gall to think of
or worse,
even do.

~ *Natalie Lasavanich, age 14*

SHANXI RIVER

Two stately behemoths fling ash to the sky.
The residue of hopes and dreams, it drifts downward
　　　to cover the land in black dust.
The coal plant will solve all problems,
Luxury beckons, all troubles seem over,
But the shimmering of the waters betrays the falseness
　　　of the image.
Peering down, the water deepens to a dark gray.
A bottle floats by, the faint outline of a fish.
A boy dips in his line, holds his rod of bamboo,
The quiet river of Shanxi moves on.

~ *Michael Zhang, age 14*

AL ALKHDHAR, THE GREEN WADI

A bright yellow sun rises in the east
To unveil a new work of art.
Splashes of green grass and red flowers now color
The landscape of yesterday's dusty dull brown.
A cascade of water washes away
All trace of grime from the last months' hard toil.
Bubbling and singing,
It dances from shiny rock to shiny rock.
The water expresses the land's joy.
It celebrates the return of life to a dry, dead desert.
The crystal white droplets sprayed from a short waterfall
Purify the air, erasing yesterday entirely.
A new era has dawned on this land,
for life has returned to the *wadi*.

~ *ElizaBeth Scott, age 16*

A GIRL WITH FLOWERS
Fidan Magerramova, age 7

VISION OF A RIVER

Do you think that
the river flows,
because someone says:
"River flow now"?
Do you think that
the elements do
what they are supposed to do
and not what they want to do?
If you think so,
then you will never see
and understand what I mean
when I say,
I will be free!

I want to be
free
like a river—
uncontrollable and wild.
I want to be
fast and dangerous
like the rapids and currents
in the river.
I want to be
like a river
with its different
shades and colors.
I want to be
natural
like a river
in its savagery.

~ *Nadja Awad, age 15*

276

RIVER II

Last night I ran like a river would
Rushing over rocky paths and silent watchers in the dark.
I cannot say I got too far
But my heart feels justified by the rush.
Like the echo of the river that rings in my ears
My mind had stopped running long before my legs did.
Like the river I let blindness lead my way
Like the hunched earth comforting the river
Along its path to endless vast spaces.
I am the whispering tree as you pass
I am the whistling wind at your window
I am free . . .

~ *Zena Sallam, age 18*

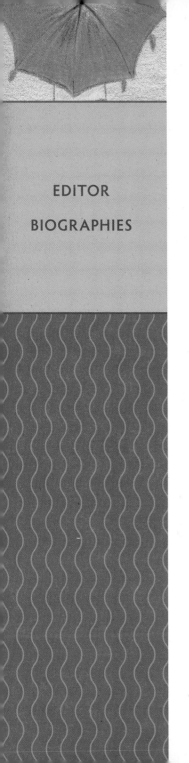

Watershed activist, writer, and radio producer PAMELA MICHAEL has spent decades working to integrate environmental and arts education into the lives of children and their communities. Cofounder, with Robert Hass, of the much-honored River of Words organization, her *Watershed Explorer* curriculum has been used to train thousands of teachers, park rangers, youth leaders, and other educators how to connect kids to their watersheds and their imaginations, inspiring them to create stunning art and poetry. She has served as the organization's executive director since its founding in 1995.

Her collection of children's work, *River of Words: Images and Poetry in Praise of Water,* won the 2003 Skipping Stones Award for Best Nature or Ecology Book. A member of the award-winning Wild Writing Women, Michael has taught writing and poetry to both children and adults, throughout the United States and abroad. She is the travel editor for San Francisco Bay Area's KPFA-FM, the first listener-supported radio station in the country, and wrote and produced a four-hour series on Buddhism in the United States, narrated by Richard Gere. Michael lives in the Curry Creek watershed on the eastern slope of Mount Diablo in northern California.

ROBERT HASS, US Poet Laureate from 1995 to 1997 and a cofounder of River of Words, is a professor of English at the University of California, Berkeley. His books of poetry include *Field Guide, Praise, Human Wishes,* and *Sun Under Wood,* and he has published a book of essays on poetry, *Twentieth Century Pleasures.* In 1997, he was named Educator of the Year by the North American Association on Environmental Education. He won the National Book Award for Poetry in 2007 for his book, *Time and Materials.*

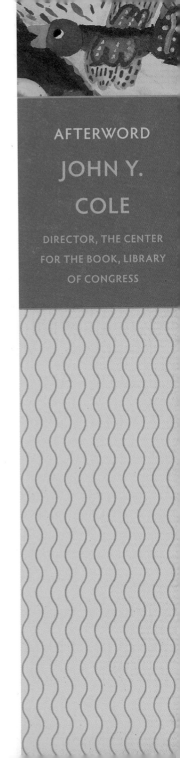

The Center for the Book in the Library of Congress is a proud River of Words partner and a frequent host of the River of Words annual awards ceremony.

River of Words and the Center for the Book are natural partners. Each organization encourages creativity among young people and uses words and imagination to do so. Both also are concerned with the importance of place and local setting, outreach, and—by involving youngsters in grassroots education projects—with encouraging life-long literacy.

There are other direct and personal connections. In 1995 Librarian of Congress James H. Billington named poet Robert Hass as the US Poet Laureate. Between 1995 and 1997, Robert and writer Pamela Michael created River of Words. During these years the three of us met, and I soon realized that their goal for River of Words fit well with the Center for the Book's mission and future hopes. The Center for the Book signed on.

A few years later, I learned that Jane Rogers, the co-chair of River of Words' board of directors, was the daughter of a man I had known and admired in the mid-1960s during my first years at The Library of Congress. These strands came together for me in the dedication of an earlier, handsome book: *River of Words: Images and Poetry in Praise of Water,* edited by Pamela Michael and published in 2003 by Heyday Books. The dedication was to Jane's father, the former Library of Congress division chief I had known several decades ago: "In memory of George A. Pughe, Jr., who loved children, believed in the value of education, and devoted his professional life to the people and programs of The Library of Congress, where River of Words was born."

Congress created the Center for the Book in 1977 as a public-private partnership to use the resources and prestige of The Library of Congress to stimulate public interest in books, reading, and literacy. To fulfill this mission the Center has gradually developed three networks of organizational partners: state Centers for the Book in each of the fifty US states plus the District of Columbia; more than eighty nonprofit organizations, including River of Words, that share our broad goals; and a growing number of international partnerships with both nonprofit and governmental organizations in other countries, particularly Russia and South Africa.

Last year the Center for the Book was privileged to host the twelfth annual awards ceremony for River of Words winners and finalists. For the first time, the ceremony was held in the Library's magnificent Thomas Jefferson Building, the first Library of Congress building. It was an appropriate setting. Thomas Jefferson, the Library's principal founder, believed in education, the active mind, and the importance of the free, unhampered pursuit of truth by an informed and involved citizenry. So does River of Words.

ACKNOWLEDGMENTS

*Y*ears ago I met Emilie Buchwald, publisher emeritus of Milkweed Editions (although I don't think she was "emeritus" at the time), in an airport. We began chatting and, as I am wont to do, I bent her ear about River of Words. She remarked that Milkweed's focus was very similar to our own—a belief in the transformative power of the arts and the importance of exploring our relationship to the natural world. She gave me her card and suggested we might want to submit something for publication but—lost in the crazy pace of River of Words's early days (not that it's any slower now)—I never followed up.

In 2006, I was given a second chance when I met Milkweed's editor in chief, Daniel Slager, at a conference in Austin, Texas. I mentioned to him that I'd always thought Milkweed would be the perfect publisher for River of Words and told him of my earlier meeting with Milkweed's founder. He gave me his card, and this time I didn't let the opportunity slip away. I sent him a manuscript of the best of our children's poems and artwork from over the years. To our joy, the manuscript was accepted.

Daniel and editors Ben Barnhart and Jim Cihlar have been skillful, sensitive, and ever-helpful in crafting this book, and understanding in the extreme about my need to juggle a demanding schedule at River of Words with my work on the manuscript. Much gratitude to them, copy editor Amy McCann, to the rest of the Milkweed staff, and to Emilie, for making this book the beautiful gift from—and to—the children of the world, as well as to the rest of us, that it is. Thank you, too, to Susan Sarratt, River of Words outreach manager, and John Oliver Simon, from Poetry Inside Out, for their assistance, and to Louisiana teachers Connie MacDonald (River of Words 2006 Teacher of the Year) and Harriet Maher, who helped us produce a Teaching Guide for this book. Connie, Harriet, and John have utilized River of Words in the classroom for many years. Their experiences and ideas have helped us refine and improve our program. Indeed, it is through

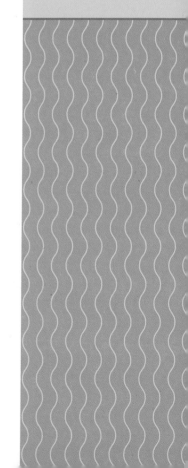

the passion and effort of thousands of teachers worldwide that River of Words succeeds.

Nonprofit organizations rely, for the most part, on the kindness of strangers. River of Words' work for the last twelve years has been supported by many people—annual donors, folks who buy prints and books from us over the Internet, those who attend our events or visit our Young at Art Gallery in Berkeley—whose faces we will never see. Along with these kind and generous strangers, we've been helped by people we do get to know a bit: donors who've become friends of the organization. These donors, along with several foundations whose funding has been critical to our success—and, in some cases, to our survival—have made it possible for us to enrich the lives of countless children, their teachers and communities. Thank you to all of them, especially key donors Paul Strasburg, Mudge Schink, Ray Lifchez, Jim and Wileta Burch, Jane Rogers and Michael Fischer, Steven Nightingale, and Arthur Kern. Thank you, too, to all the foundations that believed in our mission and helped us refine and deliver our programs over time, most especially The Geraldine R. Dodge Foundation, San Francisco Foundation, The Richard and Rhoda Goldman Fund, Center for Ecoliteracy, Panta Rhea, and the Compton Foundation.

INDEX OF

POEMS

AND ART

BY BIOREGION

Organized alphabetically by child's last name within each bioregion (please note: poems have been assigned to bioregion based on the subject of the poem, which is not necessarily the bioregion in which the poet lives)

Format:
Title of Poem / Title of Art
Poet's Name
City, State, Country (for international works)

Schools and Organizations represented in this book, organized alpha-betically by school or organization name within each state or country

Format:
School or Organization
City, State, Country (for international schools)
Teacher(s)

UNITED STATES

ALABAMA

Pelham High School
Helena, Alabama
Teacher: Connie Nolen

ARIZONA

Desert Winds Elementary School
Tucson, Arizona
Teacher: Jane Wood

Madison School
Phoenix, Arizona
Teacher: Errol Zimmerman

North High School
Phoenix, Arizona
Teacher: Marilyn Buehler

Pueblo Gardens Poetry Club
Tucson, Arizona
Teacher: Molly McKesson

Surrey Garden Christian School
Gilbert, Arizona
Teacher: Jeff Stultz

CALIFORNIA

All Saints' Episcopal Day School
Carmel, California
Teacher: Susan Goldsborough

Allendale Elementary School
Pasadena, California
Teacher: Ms. Aglilo

Anderson Valley Elementary School
Booneville, California
Teacher: Kate Dougherty

Argonne Elementary School
San Francisco, California

Berkeley High School
Berkeley, California
Teacher: Becky Gross

Bijou Community School
South Lake Tahoe, California
Teachers: Meg Knox, Sarah Knox, and Linda Loughrin

Bolinas Stinson School
Bolinas, California
Teacher: Cathy Nichelini

Carondelet High School
Concord, California
Teacher: Ms. Pasternak

Carthay Center Elementary
Norwalk, California
Teacher: Jeanine Andrade

Cragmont School
Berkeley, California
Teacher: John Oliver Simon
    (Poetry Inside Out)

The Crowden School
Berkeley, California
Teacher: John Oliver Simon
    (Poetry Inside Out)

Dolores Huerto Learning
    Academy
Oakland, California
Teachers: Elana Cassara and
    John Oliver Simon (Poetry
    Inside Out)

Edward M. Downer
    Elementary School
Richmond, California
Teacher: John Oliver Simon
    (Poetry Inside Out)

Elmwood School
Berkeley, California
Teacher: Julie Auer

Greenwood School
Mill Valley, California
Teacher: Devika Brandt
    (2004 River of Words
    Teacher of the Year)

Hawthorne School
Oakland, California
Teacher: John Oliver Simon
    (Poetry Inside Out)

Hoover Middle School
San Francisco, California
Teacher: Michael Ray (Poetry
    Inside Out)

Janesville Union School
Janesville, California
Teacher: Ms. Pastor

Kent Middle School
Kent, California
Teacher: Peter Gavin
    (2001 River of Words
    Teacher of the Year)

La Ballona Star School
Paramount, California
Teacher: Cynthia Perez-
    Jackson

Lakeshore School
San Francisco, California
Teacher: Grace Grafton
    (1998 River of Words
    Teacher of the Year)

Linscott Charter School
Watsonville, California
Teachers: Margaret Knox
    Baum, Linda Cover (2007
    River of Words Teacher of
    the Year), Robin Higbee,
    and Jody Louderback

Lowell High School
San Francisco, California
Teachers: Terri Bookwalter,
    Staci Carney, Tim Lamarre,
    Susan Terence (California
    Poets in the School), and
    Bissa Zamboldi

Marin Homeschoolers'
    Poetry Group
Fairfax, California
Teacher: Devika Brandt
    (2004 River of Words
    Teacher of the Year)

Montessori Family School
Kensington, California
Teacher: Jane Wechsler

Mt. Madonna School
Gilroy, California

Nueva School
Hillsborough, California
Teacher: Carlo Cerruti

Prospect Sierra School
El Cerrito, California
Teachers: Lucia Hecht and
    Judith Stronach

Riverside Drive
    Elementary School
Sherman Oaks, California
Teacher: Wendy Arnell

San Benito High School
Hollister, California
Teacher: John Robrock

San Domenico Upper School
San Anselmo, California
Teacher: Hilary Staples

Schafer Park School
Hayward, California
Teacher: Becky Hemann

School of the Arts
San Francisco, California
Teachers: Jim LeCuyer and
    Heather Woodward

Watsonville Charter
    School of the Arts
Watsonville, California
Teachers: Linda Cover
    (2007 River of Words
    Teacher of the Year),
    Jennifer Gill, Kulana
    Kamahao, and Rita Uribe

Woodside Elementary
    School
Woodside, California
Teacher: Kelly Corcoran

COLORADO

Mrachek Middle School
Aurora, Colorado
Teacher: Linda Johnson

Slate River School
Crested Butte, Colorado
Teacher: Sue Wilson

West Woods
    Elementary School
Arvada, Colorado
Teacher: Jennifer Arzberger

DISTRICT OF COLUMBIA

National Cathedral School
Washington, DC
Teachers: Kay Dunkley and
    Katherine Guyton

River Terrace Elementary
    School
Washington, DC
Teacher: Patricia Ann Good-
    night

Stuart Hobson School
Washington, DC
Teacher: Sandra Jenkins

FLORIDA

Fruitvale Elementary School
Sarasota, Florida
Teacher: Lauren Johnson

Scenic Heights Elementary
    School
Pensacola, Florida
Teacher: Ms. McWaters

GEORGIA

A.R. Johnson High School
Augusta, Georgia
Teacher: Audrey Smith

Barnwell Elementary School
Alpharetta, Georgia
Teachers: Danelle Chereck
    and Debbie Crider

Chamblee Charter High
    School
Chamblee, Georgia
Teachers: Diane Lynn Farmer
    and Diane Shearer

North Gwinnett High School
Suwanee, Georgia
Teacher: John Bush

Parkview High School
Lilburn, Georgia
Teacher: Mary Lynn Huie

ILLINOIS
Westmont, Illinois
Teacher: Naiying Wang Davis

INDIANA

Fang's Art School
West Lafayette, Indiana
Teacher: C.J. Fang

IOWA

Decorah High School
Decorah, Iowa
Teacher: Lamy Berland

KANSAS

**Manhattan High School
East Campus**
Manhattan, Kansas
Teachers: Ms. Converse and
Ms. Denney

LOUISIANA

Acadiana High School
Lafayette, Louisiana
Teachers: Caroline Ancelot
and Elizabeth Nehrbass

**Broadmoor Middle Magnet
School**
Baton Rouge, Louisiana
Teachers: Wes Dannreuther,
Dianne Edouard and Alan
Morton

Glasgow Middle School
Baton Rouge, Louisiana
Teacher: Geeta Dave

L.J. Alleman Middle School
Lafayette, Louisiana
Teachers: Andrée Elder, Har-
riet Maher and Charles
Mire

**Louisiana State University
Lab School**
Baton Rouge, Louisiana
Teachers: Connie McDon-
ald (2006 River of Words
Teacher of the Year) and
Candence Robillard

MAINE

**Center for Teaching
and Learning**
Edgecomb, Maine
Teachers: Nancie Atwell and
Marianne Williams

North Yarmouth Academy
Newcastle, Maine
Teacher: Ross Markonish

MICHIGAN

**Gwinn Area Community
Schools**
Skandia, Michigan
Teacher: Amy Laitinen

Home School
Laingsburg, Michigan

North Sashabaw Elementary
Clarkston, Michigan
Teacher: Ms. Pitser

**Pine Knob Elementary
School**
Clarkston, Michigan
Teachers: Ms. Allen, Paula
Boehman, Marilyn Brown,
and Beth Gifford

MISSISSIPPI

All Saints' Episcopal School
Vicksburg, Mississippi
Teacher: Greg Sellers (2002
River of Words Teacher of
the Year)

Clarkston High School
Clarkston, Mississippi
Teacher: Ms. Denstaedt

Culkin Elementary School
Vicksburg, Mississippi
Teacher: Brenda Thurman

MISSOURI

**North Kirkwood
Middle School**
Kirkwood, Missouri
Teacher: Melissa Banjak

West Junior High School
Columbia, Missouri
Teacher: Linda Durand

MONTANA

Home School
Bozeman, Montana
Teacher: Nan Darham

NEBRASKA

Chase County High School
Imperial, Nebraska
Teacher: Shelly Clark

NEVADA

Lake Tahoe School
Incline Village, Nevada
Teacher: Mia Andler

NEW HAMPSHIRE

Home School
North Hampton,
   New Hampshire
Teacher: Tammy Irving

South Meadow School
Peterborough,
   New Hampshire
Teacher: Sue Morash

NEW JERSEY

Holmdel High School
Holmdel, New Jersey
Teachers: Joan Cichalski
   and Sandra Whitten

**Student Conservation
   Association**
Newark, New Jersey
Facilitator: Ms. Bartlett

**Wheatcroft Academy
   (Home School)**
Stewartsville, New Jersey
Teacher: Valerie Blease

NEW MEXICO

Charter School 37
Santa Fe, New Mexico
Teacher: Annie Haven
   McDonnell

McCoy Elementary School
Aztec, New Mexico
Teacher: Diane Mittler

Santa Fe Preparatory School
Santa Fe, New Mexico
Teacher: Rob Wilder

NEW YORK

Brighton High School
Rochester, New York
Teacher: Karen Flynn

Vails Gate High School
New Windsor, New York
Teacher: Barbara Oliver

Ward Melville High School
Setauket, New York
Teacher: Faith Krinsky

OHIO

**Notre Dame Elementary
   School**
Portsmouth, Ohio
Teacher: Wanda Dengel

West Geauga Middle School
Chesterland, Ohio
Teacher: Michelle Gabram

OREGON

Home School
Bend, Oregon
Teacher: Kathryn Cox

**John Jacob Astor
   Elementary School**
Astoria, Oregon
Teacher: Tom Wilson

Roosevelt Middle School
Eugene, Oregon
Teacher: Gloria Merriam

Sunriver Preparatory School
Bend, Oregon
Teachers: Vicki Ball and
   Ashley Kaneda

**Three Rivers Elementary
   School**
Sunriver, Oregon
Teacher: Button Gaviglio

PENNSYLVANIA

Abington Friends School
Jenkintown, Pennsylvania
Teachers: Anne Fields and
   Jane McVeigh-Schultz

Arthur Street School
Hazelton, Pennsylvania
Teacher: Marilyn Hazelton

Fulton Elementary School
Lancaster, Pennsylvania
Teacher: Barbara Strasko

RHODE ISLAND

**Brown University—River of
   Words Outreach Program**
Providence, Rhode Island
Facilitators: Lucas Foglia,
   Allyse Heartwell and Ryan
   Tierney

Hope High School
Providence, Rhode Island
Teacher: Rachel Moran

UTAH

Brighton High School
Salt Lake City, Utah
Teacher: Patricia Russell
    (1997 River of Words
    Teacher of the Year)

VIRGINIA

J Art Studio
Lorton, Virginia
Teacher: Ju Yun

WASHINGTON

Lakeside Middle School
Seattle, Washington
Teachers: Alicia Hokanson
    (2003 River of Words
    Teacher of the Year),
    Lance King, and Kim-An
    Lieberman

WISCONSIN

River Ridge Middle School
Bloomington, Wisconsin
Teacher: Barb Neises

INTERNATIONAL

AFGHANISTAN

Shamman Art
Quetta, Pakistan
Teacher: Hassan Ali Hatif

AZERBAIJAN

Palace of Children and
    Youth Creative Work
    after Tofig Ismailov
Baku, Azerbaijan
Teacher: Tatyana Kesa

BANGLADESH

American International
    School
Dhaka, Bangladesh
Teacher: Amy Shawver

BULGARIA

Cot Color & Co.
Sofia, Bulgaria
Teacher: Tsonka Voyvodova

EGYPT

Cairo American School
Cairo, Egypt
Teacher: Mark Pleasants

ENGLAND

Harthill Primary School
Harthill, Sheffield, England
Teacher: John McKay

INDONESIA

Yogyakarta, Indonesia
Teacher: Yuni Purnamawati

IRAN

Tehran, Iran
Teacher: Nahal Bahreman

MALAYSIA

SK Convent
Perak, Malaysia
Teacher: Ancy Ng

CHINA

American International
    School of Guangzhou
Guangzhou, China
Teacher: Amy Shawver

Simply Art
Hong Kong, China
Teachers: Hoo Cheong Lau
    and Chui Fan Lee

PHILIPPINES

**Philippine Sun Yat
  High School**
Manila, Philippines
Teacher: William Lee

St. Jude Catholic School
Manila, Philippines
Teacher: Olivia Dunes

St. Stephens High School
Manila, Philippines
Teacher: Rommel Quimson

TAIWAN

Taipei American School
Taipei, Taiwan
Teacher: Megan Pettigrew

THAILAND

**New International School of
  Thailand**
Bangkok, Thailand
Teacher: Nicholas Daniel

UKRAINE
Zhytomyr, Ukraine
Teacher: Anne Ivchenko

YEMEN

Sana'a International School
Sana'a, Yemen
Teacher: Dan Summers

MORE BOOKS FROM MILKWEED EDITIONS

The Stories from Where We Live Series

Edited by Sara St. Antoine
Literary field guides to the places we call home.

The California Coast

The Great Lakes

The Great North American Prairie

The Gulf Coast

The North Atlantic Coast

The South Atlantic Coast and Piedmont

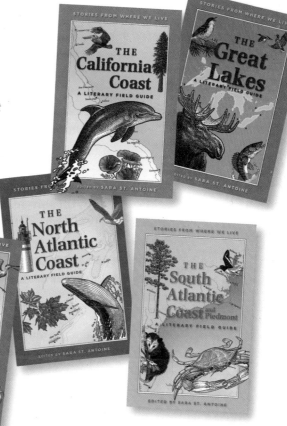

MILKWEED EDITIONS

Founded in 1979, Milkweed Editions is one of the largest indepen-
dent, nonprofit literary publishers in the United States. Milkweed
publishes with the intention of making a humane impact on society,
in the belief that good writing can transform the human heart and
spirit. Within this mission, Milkweed publishes in four areas: fiction,
nonfiction, poetry, and children's literature for middle-grade readers.

JOIN US

Milkweed depends on the generosity of foundations and individu-
als like you, in addition to the sales of its books. In an increasingly
consolidated and bottom-line-driven publishing world, your support allows us to select and publish books on the basis of their literary quality and the depth of their message. Please visit our Web site
(www.milkweed.org) or contact us at (800) 520-6455 to learn more
about our donor program.

STUDY GUIDE

Please visit www.milkweed.org for more information on this and
other titles, including a study guide for *River of Words*.

Interior design by Cathy Spengler
Typeset in LinoLetter by Cathy Spengler
Printed on acid-free Rolland paper
by Friesens Corporation